TASTE
for
TRUTH

A 30 DAY
WEIGHT LOSS BIBLE STUDY

TASTE
for
TRUTH

BARB RAVELING

TRUTHWAY PRESS

Truthway Press
First Edition 2013
Second Edition 2017
Third Edition 2017

The second edition of this book contains only minor edits. The third edition is exactly like the second except for the interior design. If you're teaching a class, you can easily use any edition in the same class. Just be aware that the page numbers on the third edition will be different than the first and second edition because of the new interior design.

All scripture quotations, unless otherwise indicated, are taken from the New American Standard Bible ®, Copyright © 1960, 1962, 1963, 1968, 1971, 1972, 1973, 1975, 1977, 1995 by the Lockman Foundation. Used by permission.

www.Lockman.org

This book is not intended as a substitute for the advice of professional counselors or physicians. Please seek professional help if you're struggling with an eating disorder and get advice from your doctor or dietician before starting a weight loss plan if you have health issues.

The names of the people in the stories of this book have been changed to protect their privacy.

ISBN: 0-9802243-1-4
ISBN-13: 978-0-9802243-1-3

To Heidi.
Thanks for being such a great encourager.

Acknowledgements

SPECIAL THANKS TO my husband for all his wonderful and wise counsel with the editing of this book.

A very special thanks to all the ladies who helped me test the study and provide feedback: Heidi, Adriane, Carrie, Sara, Teri, Susan, Pam, Vanya, Linda, Dawn, Debbie, Holly, Martha, Polly, Glenda, Ginger, Maureen, Jenny, Lisa, Rita, and Shawna. I appreciate all of you!

Thanks also to Heidi Bylsma for teaching my 15-day weight loss Bible study on your blog, encouraging me along the way, and just for being a wonderful friend. I appreciate you!

Contents

Introduction

*W*OULDN'T IT BE nice if we could just say a little prayer—*Please help me lose weight, God*—then go to sleep and wake up the next day skinny? Unfortunately, God doesn't usually work that way. Instead, He wants us to get involved in our own transformation.

That's not easy because many of us have a stronghold of emotional eating. In the Old Testament, a stronghold was a physical fortress that people went to for protection from the enemy. A stronghold was also a spiritual place of protection.

David often referred to God as his stronghold because he was in the habit of running to God for refuge. Just read the Psalms. Over and over, we see David going to God to talk over his problems with Him.

This is God's desire for us, as well. He wants us to go to Him for help with life. But it's so much easier to turn to other things, including food. When we run to food too often, it becomes our place of refuge—a stronghold—but not a good one.

This stronghold is built on lies. Lies like *This will make me feel better.* Or *I should be able to eat what I want when I want.* Or *Life will be boring if I have to restrict my eating long-term.*

It takes a lot of work to get those lies out of our system. We can't do it by merely following a weight loss plan because a weight loss plan only controls behavior. It doesn't rid us of the lies that fuel our behavior.

If we want to eliminate those lies, we'll need to do what the Bible tells us to do: renew our minds (Romans 12:2). As we take off the lies that make us want to eat too much and put on the truth that sets us free, our desires will change. We'll actually *want* to eat with control.

Taste for Truth offers thirty days of renewing-the-mind help. Each day covers a different aspect of the journey of breaking free from the control of food.

The first six lessons are all about boundaries. It's important to do those lessons in order because they lay the foundation for the rest of the study. If things are going smoothly, go through the remaining lessons in the order given. However, if you reach the point where you're tired of your weight loss plan and want to quit (this often happens around Day 6 or 7), skip ahead to a lesson that deals with what you're struggling with. Following are a few suggestions:

- If you feel like eating everything in sight, go to Day 4, 19, 21, 23, or 26.

- If you're discouraged or feel like quitting, go to Day 3, 8, 13, 17, 22, 29, or 30.

- If you feel like you should be able to eat what you want when you want, go to Day 5, 7, 10, or 27.

- If you have a bad weigh-in or feel like you *have* to be skinny, go to Day 11, 12, 13 or 28.

- If you can't make yourself renew your mind, go to Day 15 or Appendix C.

Beginning on Day 15, I'll ask you to add the free app *I Deserve a Donut (And Other Lies That Make You Eat)* to your renewing-the-mind routine. You can use this resource throughout your life to say no to temptation and to talk over life with God. It's also available in paperback and e-book format.

If you don't have *I Deserve a Donut*, you can find many of the questions and Bible verses from the book at barbraveling.com by using the search box on the right side of the blog.

My prayer is that God will use this study to help you break free from the stronghold of overeating and grow closer to Him in the process. I'm excited to see what He'll do in your life as you go to Him for help with weight loss. Are you ready to begin? Let's get started!

Day 1

The Secret to Losing Weight and Keeping It Off

DO YOU EVER feel like you'll *never* break free from the control of food? I used to feel that way. Overeating was that one thing in life I thought I'd never be able to overcome. Every year, I'd make the same New Year's resolution: *Lose x number of pounds.* Every year I failed to reach my goal.

I tried diets. And about every twenty-ninth time they worked— usually when I had some reason I absolutely had to lose weight. A wedding. A reunion. Or a number on the scale so shocking I could hardly believe what I was seeing.

If I was beyond-the-end-of-my-rope desperate, I could some-times work up enough willpower to lose weight. At least enough to get me into the "good enough" category.

But it never lasted. I always gained the weight back. This went on for twenty-five years. Gain. Lose. Gain. Lose. Gain. Lose. I could pretty much tell what my life was like by looking at my weight. When life was good, I was slim. When life was bad, I was over-weight. I was an emotional eater, and my weight reflected what was going on in my life at the time.

I wish I could say, "But then one day, I saw the light and sud-denly my life changed!"

Unfortunately, that's not what happened. This is what really happened: One day I discovered a discipline that God has used to transform my life in countless ways. That discipline is the

14

renewing of the mind. And because of the Holy Spirit working through that discipline, I now live free from the control of food.

However—and this is a sad however—it didn't happen overnight. It took a long time. Hours of meeting with God to discuss my food issues with Him and look at life from His perspective. But those hours spent with Him? They were incredible hours. Hours that brought me closer to Him. Hours that got me excited about His Word. And hours that slowly, but powerfully, began to change me.

If you're in the same spot I was for twenty-five years—feeling like you'll never break free from food's control over you—let me encourage you. God is powerful. He can do anything, including setting you free from the stronghold of overeating. He may not do it as quickly as you'd like—that's almost a guarantee—but He will do it if you seek Him for help. This Bible study is all about going to Him for help. Let's begin by getting a biblical view of transformation.

BIBLE STUDY

1. Read the following Bible verses with weight loss in mind. List the role we play and the role God plays in the transformation process.

	Our Role	God's Role
John 8:31-32		
John 15:1-5		

Romans 12:2		
2 Corinthians 10:3-5		

2. In summary, what is our part in the transformation process?

3. What is God's part in the transformation process?

4. What do you normally do when you want to be transformed in the area of weight?

5. According to the verses you just read, is that enough? Why or why not?

The Greek word used for "abide" in John 8:31-32 and John 15:4-5 is the same word that's used for living in a house. The idea is that we don't just visit the Word for ten minutes a day. We *live* in the Word. Meditate on it. Chew on it as we walk through the day.

Let it fill us and change the way we think about life. Let it fill us and change the way we think about food. And even let it fill us and change the way we think about ourselves.

My prayer is that this Bible study will be a time of deep fellowship with God as you go to Him for help with weight loss and maintenance. Each day I'll have a short study and an optional assignment that will help you apply the lesson. Here's your first assignment.

ASSIGNMENT

1. Buy a journal you can use for this study and download the free app *I Deserve a Donut (And Other Lies That Make You Eat)* if you haven't already done so. You can read more about this resource in the introduction to this book. It's also available as a paperback or e-book.

2. Practice abiding in God. Set a timer for fifteen minutes and just sit down with Him. Listen to Him. Talk to Him. Meditate on His Word. Enjoy Him. Worship Him.

Day 2

The Quick and Easy
Approach to Weight Loss

*T*HE FIRST TIME I taught a weight loss Bible study, I went in expecting it to be like a weight loss class, something I was well familiar with after years of dieting. It didn't take long to find out that a weight loss Bible study is a lot different than a weight loss class.

First of all, it was a lot more fun. The women were gregarious, the discussions were lively, and the only dark spot on the horizon was that we felt compelled to skip the traditional Bible study treat. It was a relief to share both our eating and non-eating struggles and go to the Bible for help—things you don't usually get to do at a weight loss class.

But there was one major drawback: When you go to a weight loss class, you come in prepared to sacrifice. You know you have to follow their restrictive eating plan, and you've already made the emotional commitment to follow it. You're prepared to suffer.

This isn't true with a weight loss Bible study. In some ways, the Bible study itself makes us less likely to commit to an eating plan. Because in the back of our minds we're holding out hope that maybe this Bible study will be the answer to all our problems, and we won't have to cut down on our eating.

If only this were true. I would so love to find that quick and easy approach to permanent weight loss. Here's the sad, sad truth: This book is not the easy answer to weight loss. If you want to lose weight *and* keep it off, you'll need to do two things: **renew** your mind and **restrict** your eating. Not just for the duration of the Bible study, but for life.

Yes, I said it. Life. If I had gone to a weight loss Bible study 15 years ago, that is *not* what I would have wanted to hear. In those days I was a big fan of the quick and easy approach. Just tell me what to do, make it fun, and I'm there. If you want me to cut out some calories for awhile, I'm game. But I'm sure not going to restrict myself for life.

But here's the thing. God often tells us to restrict things for life. He's not all about "do what you want when you want." On the contrary, God is all about "love me with all your heart, soul, mind, and strength." One of the ways we love Him well is to hold His gifts with open hands, willing to give them up if they get in the way of loving Him.

Lifelong Boundaries

We'll talk about the spiritual benefits of boundaries later, but today I want to look at the practical benefits. In the past, it never occurred to me to restrict my eating when I wasn't on a diet. On the contrary, non-diet life was my opportunity to live it up—to eat *what* I wanted *when* I wanted without regard for the consequences.

It took me awhile to figure out that that was a bad way to live life. That life was actually *better* when I ate with control. I don't know why it took so long. After all, I exercised control in other areas of my life: I was faithful to my husband. I paid off my credit card each month. I didn't say every single little thing that popped into my mind. So why not exercise control with eating? Not just when I was on a diet, but all the time? In other words, lifelong boundaries in the area of food.

According to freedictionary.com, a boundary is *something that indicates a border or limit.* A playground fence is an example of a boundary. It limits where the kids can play, but that's not all it does. It also cramps their style.

Those little kids would love to run out in the street and look at all those fun, noisy cars—but the fence holds them in and says, "No, kids, you can't play in the street." That doesn't mean the fence is bad. On the contrary, the fence makes their lives better because it protects them from harm.

The same is true for us. Lifelong boundaries in the area of food make our lives better because they keep us safe. Yes, they cramp our style, but you know what? Our style needs to be cramped because there are consequences to eating what we want when we want.

Here are a few of them: Clothes that don't fit. Discomfort. Diabetes. Sore joints. Weight gain. Depression. Heart disease. Hopelessness. Lack of energy. An early death. These are just a few of the enemies that lurk outside the "fence" of our boundaries waiting to destroy us.

There are several ways to limit eating long-term. If you already have lifelong boundaries, great, you're set to go. If you don't and you'd like to consider setting some, check out Appendix A in the back of this book. Today's study will focus on the practical benefits of lifelong boundaries.

PERSONAL EVALUATION

1. Do you have boundaries in any other areas of your life? If so, what areas? Be specific.

2. Why do you have boundaries in those areas of your life? Why not just do whatever you feel like doing?

3. Do you have lifelong boundaries in the area of food? If so, what are they?

4. What happens when you eat "what you want when you want" on a regular basis? List as many consequences as possible.

5. Would lifelong boundaries in the area of food make your life better or worse? Explain.

6. What would you have to sacrifice to follow lifelong boundaries?

7. What do you sacrifice when you live a life *without* boundaries?

8. Why do you think we're so opposed to lifelong boundaries in the area of food when we support them in other areas of our lives?

9. What would your life look like if you were to have boundaries in place all the time?

10. Do you think God wants you to have boundaries in the area of food? Why or why not?

ASSIGNMENT

We're taking the quick and easy approach to assignments today. No assignment!

I'll Start Tomorrow

I'M AT THE Dairy Queen drive-through, waiting for my blizzard—my final good-bye to indulgence before I start getting serious about my boundaries. I was planning to start today, but there was a glitch.

A friend asked me to go to the bakery, and I had a frappe. *No problem,* I thought. *I'll just make it my snack for the day.* But then my daughter made white chocolate chip cranberry scones for dinner. I couldn't resist a second helping. My boundaries specifically say "no second helpings."

I'll just start again tomorrow, I told myself, as I grabbed the car keys for a trip to the Dairy Queen. *Might as well have one last blizzard.*

My guess is that you've had the same experience. Why do you suppose we keep putting it off until tomorrow? Here's my theory: We do it because a) we don't really want to follow our boundaries and b) it's a wonderful opportunity to eat without guilt. Because after all, we'll be so good tomorrow!

Here are a few of the lies we tell ourselves when we're sitting at the drive-through, waiting for our last treat:

1. It will be easier tomorrow.

2. We'll feel more like sticking to our boundaries tomorrow.

3. We *will* stick to our boundaries tomorrow.

The truth is:

1. It won't be easier tomorrow.

2. We'll never feel like sticking to our boundaries if there are treats around (and there are always treats around).

3. We probably won't stick to our boundaries tomorrow if we're not willing to stick to them today.

Here's what we'll need to do if we want to break free from the control of food: develop a mindset of **always** following the boundaries. In other words, ban the phrase "I'll start tomorrow" from our vocabulary.

BIBLE STUDY

1. Often we view the night before we start following our boundaries as an opportunity to eat as much as we want. This might not be a problem if it happened once in a lifetime or even once a year. But it becomes a problem when it happens once a week or even once a day. Think of your own life. How often do you say "I'll start my boundaries tomorrow?"

2. What happens when you constantly say, "I'll start tomorrow"?

3. Do you think God would say, "Yes, eat as much as possible tonight, and tomorrow you can start being good at following your boundaries"? Why or why not?

4. What does the Bible have to say about this subject?

   a. Proverbs 25:16

   b. Romans 13:14

   c. 1 Corinthians 10:31

   d. 1 Peter 2:11

5. How would your life change if you were to ban the phrase "I'll start tomorrow" from your vocabulary and make a commitment to lifelong boundaries?

6. What would you have to sacrifice to make that commitment?

7. Do you think God wants you to make the commitment? Why or why not?

ASSIGNMENT

Spend some time talking to God about the possibility of limiting your eating, not just temporarily, but long-term. If you don't already have boundaries, read Appendix A at the back of this book.

Not Even One Bite

*I*T'S 11:30 IN the morning, and I've already broken my boundaries. Not because I was dying to eat anything. But because I wasn't trying that hard *not* to eat anything. Granted, I'm on vacation right now (typing in the car to keep from getting bored), but if I look at the past, vacation is one of those times when I most need to follow my boundaries.

The conclusion I'm coming to after six years of maintaining my weight is that I'm the sort of person who always needs to follow her boundaries. Why? Because I love to eat, I sometimes eat for emotional reasons, and I'm not opposed to eating unhealthy amounts of food.

If I were like that with alcohol, I'd be an alcoholic. And alcoholics don't take breaks from their boundaries when they go on vacation.

Let's take a look at the life of an alcoholic for a minute. What type of person is at risk for alcoholism? I can think of three types of people: 1) those who love the taste of alcohol, 2) those who turn to alcohol for emotional reasons, and 3) those who think it's fun to consume large quantities of alcohol.

Recovering alcoholics know they have to be careful. They set a rigid boundary: not even one sip. It's an accepted belief in our culture that alcoholics need boundaries. The minute they start thinking, *It's just one drink,* they're in danger.

Unfortunately, it's not an accepted belief that we need boundaries. Maybe that's because we aren't able to say, "Not even one bite." We'd starve to death. But we *can* say, "Not even one bite outside our boundaries." The question is, what kind of a person needs to set rigid boundaries with food?

I can think of three types of people: 1) those who love the taste of food, 2) those who turn to food for emotional reasons, and 3) those who think it's fun to consume large quantities of food.

Is that you? I know it's me. By nature, I'm the type of person who will mess up my life with food if left to my own devices. Because of that, I need strict boundaries. And like the alcoholic, the minute I start thinking, *It's just one bite,* I'm in danger.

BIBLE STUDY

1. Describe the life of an alcoholic who drinks whenever she feels like drinking.

2. For the sake of argument, let's say a foodaholic is a person who can't stop eating. Describe the life of a foodaholic who eats whenever she feels like eating. If this is you right now, describe your current life. (But don't get discouraged—that life is going to change!)

3. Read 1 Timothy 4:7. One of the current worldly fables is the idea that we're happiest when we do what we want when we want. The fewer rules the better. Look over your answers to the first and second question. Do you think this is true on a practical level? Why or why not?

4. Do you think you're the type of person who can eat what you want when you want without having it mess up your life? Why or why not?

5. Do you think an alcoholic could escape her alcoholism while still having a sip of alcohol here and there? Why or why not?

6. Do you think a foodaholic could escape her foodaholism while still having a bite of food here and there outside her boundaries? Why or why not?

7. What does the Bible have to say on this subject?

    a. Romans 13:14

    b. 1 Corinthians 10:31

    c. Hebrews 12:11

    d. 1 Peter 1:13-16

ASSIGNMENT

1. Spend some more time thinking and praying about the possibility of boundaries if you don't already have them. I'll ask you if you want to make a commitment to boundaries on Day 6.

2. If you're having a hard time making a decision about boundaries, use the questions in Appendix B to help you with your decision.

I Hate Boundaries

OMETIMES I FEEL like a little kid throwing a tantrum at the toy store. I want what I want—and I want it now. I'm tired of following these humdrum boundaries. I want a little excitement in my life! A nice big out-of-the-boundary treat—or maybe two or three.

Do you ever feel that way? I'd be surprised if you didn't. After all, we live in a culture that says, "Forget about the rules. Just follow your heart. Do what you feel like doing." But what if what you feel like doing is eating everything in sight?

If we want to embrace our boundaries—and even grow to love them—we'll have to get this idea that rules are bad out of our system. Paul talks about rules in 1 Timothy 1:8-9. Listen to what he says and answer the questions that follow:

> *But we know that the Law is good, if one uses it lawfully, real-izing the fact that law is not made for a righteous person, but for those who are lawless and rebellious, for the ungodly and sinners, for the unholy and profane, for those who kill their fathers or mothers, for murderers.*

1. What does Paul say about the law?

2. Who was the law made for?

3. Are you lawless and rebellious in the area of food?

Paul tells us that the law is good if we use it in the right way. He then goes on to tell us who needs the law—the rebellious and the lawless. This makes sense.

People who aren't rebellious don't need the law. They'd do the right thing even if there were no laws. It's the rebellious ones who need the law—the ones who say, "I shouldn't have to follow the law, and I won't follow it!" They need the law to protect themselves and others from their bad behavior.

I hate to say it, but we're often lawless and rebellious when it comes to food. We stomp our little feet and say, "I shouldn't have to have boundaries. I should be able to eat *what* I want *when* I want." The minute the law is removed—in other words, the minute we give up our boundaries—we're back at it, stuffing our faces with everything in sight. The truth is, we need the law to protect ourselves from our bad behavior.

BIBLE STUDY

1. Read the following Bible verses. Do they embrace the idea that we should be able to do whatever we want without restraint? If not, what do they teach?

a. Romans 13:14

b. 1 Corinthians 6:12

c. 1 Timothy 4:7b

d. James 4:6

e. 1 Peter 1:14-16

2. In summary, why might God want you to have boundaries and follow them?

3. What happens when you throw away the rules and eat whatever you want?

4. Do you want that to happen? Explain.

5. If not, what will you need to do to protect yourself from your "rebellious and lawless" nature?

ASSIGNMENT

Choose two or three Bible verses from today's lesson to memorize. Write the Bible verses on index cards so you can refer back to them.

Day 6

That Scary First Step

WE'VE TALKED A lot about boundaries the last couple of days. Today I'm going to ask you to consider setting your own boundaries if you haven't already done that. Here's why: because I know from personal experience how easy it is to put off making decisions. I do it all the time.

That said, I also know how hard it is to make a commitment, especially when you know it's going to require a sacrifice. So how do you come to the point where you're willing to say, "I'm going to make a commitment to follow boundaries *for the rest of my life*"?

Just writing those words scares me—even though I've already made the commitment. There's no doubt—it's going to be a sacrifice. But it's also going to be an incredible blessing. You just may not be able to see the blessing at this point.

Several things keep us from making a commitment to lifelong boundaries. Let's look at a few of those things before you make your decision. Here are six reasons we don't want lifelong boundaries.

REASONS WE DON'T WANT **BOUNDARIES**

1. We want to eat.

The first reason is plain and simple: We love food, and we don't want to limit ourselves. If this is why you don't want boundaries, make a list in your journal of what your life looks like *with* boundaries and *without* boundaries. Which life is better? You may also want to look at Day 7 in this Bible study.

2. We want to keep our options open.

What if a great eating opportunity comes up and you have to miss out on it just because of your pesky old boundaries? If this is a concern for you, try this: Make a two-column chart. On the top left, write "Advantages of Keeping My Options Open." On the right, put "Disadvantages of Keeping My Options Open." Then fill in the chart. I did this and I had one advantage and about eight disadvantages. I decided it was worth having boundaries!

3. We don't like rules.

Sometimes it's not so much about the food but more about the restrictions. When we hear the word *rules*, we immediately want to break them. If this is you, review yesterday's lesson and check out the entitlement questions and verses in *I Deserve a Donut* or on my blog at barbraveling.com.

4. We're afraid of failure.

This is a toughie. It's hard to try again when we've failed so many times in the past. We don't want to get our hopes up and then be disappointed again. If you're afraid you won't be able to follow your boundaries, let me ease your mind: Of course you won't be able to follow them! At least not perfectly.

You'll break them—that's almost a guarantee—but that's okay. Because you're not set free by following your boundaries perfectly. You're set free by the renewing of your mind. Failure is an opportunity to renew your mind once again! If you're afraid of failure, read Day 17 or 28 in this study, or do the worry or perfectionism questions and Bible verses in *I Deserve a Donut* or on my blog.

5. We want to wait until after that next big eating occasion.

It's hard to make a commitment to boundaries when there's a wonderful eating occasion just around the corner. A holiday. A birthday. This month's potluck at church. If we could just get past *that* event, wouldn't it be easier to start our boundaries?

NEWS FLASH!!! An event will *always* be just around the corner. But if we're planning on lifelong boundaries, it's a moot point. Because *life* includes all of those eating occasions. Sooner or later we'll have to learn how to eat with moderation if we want to lose weight and keep it off.

If you have a big event coming up in a few days, it won't be a big deal to start your boundaries after that. But if your big event is coming up in three weeks or two months, it might be better to start right away! If you struggle with this issue, review Day 3 or try the "I'll Start Tomorrow" questions at the end of today's lesson.

6. We think we can lose weight and keep it off without boundaries.

This is a funny one. But it's what we think. Somewhere in the back of our minds, we have this hazy idea that if we just try to be "good," maybe then we'll be able to lose weight *without* restricting our eating.

Here's the sad, sad truth: Unless we a) suddenly lose our taste for food, b) stop eating for emotional reasons, or c) have a sudden change in our metabolism, we probably won't be able to lose weight and keep it off without lifelong boundaries. If you struggle with this issue, review Day 4.

BIBLE STUDY

1. Look back over the six reasons we don't want boundaries. Which reasons do you struggle with, if any?

2. Can you think of any other reasons you don't want to have boundaries?

3. If you're having a hard time committing to (or following) boundaries, take the time now to look at some of the suggestions I gave in today's lesson. There won't be a regular Bible study today so you'll have time to follow through on some of those suggestions.

CHALLENGE

If you decide to give boundaries a try, read through the following challenges and see if there's a challenge you'd be willing to commit to. Think about it. Pray about it. Then record your commitment in the space provided. Here are the challenges:

1. **Get-your-feet-wet-challenge:** Set one small boundary such as *no eating after dinner*. This is a valid option as you'll still be able to work on the renewing of the mind. Just don't make the mistake of expecting to lose weight with this challenge. You probably won't be able to lose weight unless you limit your eating for the whole day rather than just for a small part of the day.

2. **Middle-of-the-road challenge:** Set potential lifelong boundaries and commit to following them for the length of this Bible study.

3. **Hardcore challenge:** Set lifelong boundaries. This doesn't mean you can't ever change your boundaries or even loosen them up from time to time. It just means that you're setting

boundaries with the idea that you'll always have boundaries, even after you lose weight.

4. **Harder-than-hardcore challenge:** Set lifelong boundaries and ban the phrase "I'll start my boundaries tomorrow" from your vocabulary.

YOUR COMMITMENT

I will commit to the _____ challenge.

I will commit to the following boundaries:

I will begin following my boundaries on _____

I'LL START TOMORROW QUESTIONS

One of the things that has helped me follow my boundaries more than anything is to answer the "I'll Start Tomorrow" questions from *I Deserve a Donut* in my journal the first several days of a new commitment. Somehow they just help me sink the thought into my mind that "Yes, I really am going to follow these boundaries."

I've copied the questions below so you can give them a try. Go ahead and answer them now, then once a day for the next few days. It will seem like overkill, but each time you answer them, you'll be drilling important truths into your mind that will help you follow your boundaries.

1. What are your boundaries?

2. Is there ever a good (i.e. easy) time to start following your boundaries?

3. What sacrifices will you have to make to lose and/or maintain your weight?

4. Will you have to make those sacrifices no matter when you make the commitment to follow your boundaries?

5. What would you gain by starting to follow your boundaries today?

6. What do you think will happen if you don't start today? Be specific.

7. Would it be better to start following your boundaries today, or is there a good reason to wait?

8. Are you the type of person who can go without boundaries in this area of your life and still lose or maintain your weight? Why or why not?

9. Is there anything you need to accept?

10. What will your life and body look like a couple of months down the road if you develop the habit of consistently following your boundaries?

11. When you think of all you have to gain, is it worth following your boundaries today?

ASSIGNMENT

1. Write the Bible verses that you're memorizing (from yesterday's lesson) in your journal.

2. If you added boundaries to your life, write out your boundaries on an index card and put them someplace where you'll see them every day. You could tape them to your refrigerator or your bathroom mirror or just leave them as an index card in your Bible.

Day 7

I Like It. I Love It. I Want Some More Of It.

N THE BACK of my mind I have this glorious picture. I'm sitting at an outdoor café on a cobbled street in Rome, skinny as a rail, in a simple yet elegant outfit. With my Audrey Hepburn sunglasses perched on my head, I slowly turn the pages of the book I'm reading, *Sidewalk Cafes in Rome*.

As I take another sip of my cappuccino and a bite of my cream-filled cannoli, I ponder the age-old question, *What should I have for my next treat?*

There's just one little problem with this picture: It's not realistic.

Think of it. If I eat all the things I picture myself eating in this little fantasy, it won't be an elegantly thin woman sitting at that table. It will be a pleasantly plump matron. With sensible shoes, stretchy pants, and a roll of Tums in her bulky handbag.

Why? Because that woman won't be bothering herself with boundaries. She'll be eating *what* she wants *when* she wants. And when that woman eats what she wants, elegantly thin isn't what she ends up with.

IS MORE REALLY BETTER?

Let me ask you a question. Where did we get this idea that more is better? Was it from the commercials that kept telling us we needed more? Was it from the fast food restaurants that offered us a bargain if we ordered a bigger meal? Or maybe it's just from too many church potlucks with too many tasty dishes.

Whatever it is, we've picked up a lie. The only reason we think more is better is because we've chosen to completely ignore the consequences of more. Here's the truth: A little is fun. A lot is not. (It even rhymes.) In real life, "a lot" brings so many consequences with it, that it's anything but fun.

This is true on a practical level, but it's also true on a spiritual level. When we try to fill ourselves up with things that can never fill us (food, for example), we're never satisfied. We're like that leaky cistern in Jeremiah 2:13. We always want more. We'll be far better off if we hold all things with open hands—including food—and fill ourselves up with God.

BIBLE STUDY

1. If you were to eat what-you-want-when-you-want 100% of the time, how much do you think you'd weigh? (Seriously.)

2. If you were to eat what-you-want-when-you-want 100% of the time, would you be happy? Why or why not?

3. Why do you suppose we think that eating whatever we want will make us happy?

4. When the Bible says things like, "Don't love the world or the things in the world" (1 John 2:15), do you think God is just trying to ruin our fun, or does God know what's best for us? Explain.

5. What do the following Bible verses say about focusing our lives on always indulging ourselves?

   a. Proverbs 23:20-21

   b. Matthew 6:33

   c. 1 Corinthians 10:31

   d. Colossians 3:2

   e. 1 John 2:15-17

6. What will happen physically and spiritually if you focus life on always indulging yourself?

7. Is your life better with boundaries or without boundaries? Explain.

ASSIGNMENT

1. Answer the "I'll Start Tomorrow" questions from page 39 in your journal. Try not to look at the answers you gave last time as God can give you new insights each time you answer these questions.

2. Try to write the Bible verses you're memorizing in your journal without looking back at them.

Day 8

The Anatomy of a Habit

OMETIMES THE PROCESS of transformation is so slow it about drives me crazy. I think I have a habit licked and then there it is, staring me right back in the face again. It's discouraging. I hope you're not feeling discouraged right now. I know how hard it is to keep pushing on.

If you get discouraged, think of Hebrews 12:11: "All discipline for the moment seems not to be joyful, but sorrowful; yet to those who have been trained by it, *afterwards* it yields the peaceful fruit of righteousness."

During the trial, it's anything but peaceful because our desires are warring within us. They're saying, *Give up! This is too hard. You can't do it. Go get something great to eat and end this misery!*

Do you see why it's so important to take the time to renew our minds? We can't stand up against those voices for long. We need the truth of God's Word to shine in and shatter those thoughts.

So many times in the past, when I've wanted a quick fix to my problems, I've looked back later and thought, *Oh, that's why God didn't solve my problem right away. He wanted to teach me a lesson.*

God has a reason for not giving us the quick fix: He wants us to be conformed to His image, and He uses trials to help us grow. Weight loss is one of those trials. It's not fun, but God can do great things in our lives if we persevere and keep going to Him for help.

Today we'll look at six stages we go through to break free from the control of food. Try to find out where you are now and what you need to do to get to the next level. Here are the six stages:

6 STAGES OF A HABIT

1. FULLY ENTRENCHED

In this stage, you want to lose weight, but you haven't set boundaries or made a commitment to renew your mind on a daily basis.

To get to the next level: 1) Pray for the willingness to change. 2) Find out why you don't want to set boundaries. 3) Focus your renewing of the mind efforts on that area. For example, if you don't want to set boundaries because you love to eat, do the indulgence questions and Bible verses from *I Deserve a Donut* or my blog once a day. If you want boundaries, but haven't gotten around to setting them yet, do the procrastination or perfectionism questions and Bible verses.

Lies you'll need to let go of: I should be able to eat what I want when I want. Boundaries make my life worse. I don't need boundaries. If I just focus on eating healthy, I'll be able to lose weight without setting boundaries. I'll set my boundaries later.

2. WILLING, BUT NOT ABLE

In this stage, you've set your boundaries and you've made a commitment to renew your mind, but you can't make yourself follow through on one or both of your commitments.

To get to the next level: 1) Find a friend or a group to do the Bible study with. 2) Get an accountability partner to hold you accountable to the renewing of the mind. 3) Renew your mind every single time you break your boundaries. 4) Consider having a contest with a friend. Here's an example: Each time you break your boundaries, write it down, but don't tell your friend (otherwise, she might break hers). At the end of the time period whoever has the fewest "breaks" wins a prize. Prizes could be a movie, a cleaning or babysitting session, a dinner out, or whatever you can think of.

Lies you'll need to let go of: I shouldn't have to put a lot of effort into this. The renewing of the mind doesn't work. Exercise is more important than the renewing of the mind, and I don't have time for both. I can do this in my own strength. I'll never change anyway, so why bother?

3. WILLING AND ABLE

In this stage, you're renewing your mind on a regular basis. You're making progress—but you may not *think* you're making progress because you keep breaking your boundaries. A lot of people give up at this stage. Don't do that! It takes awhile for the truth to kick in and start changing your behavior long-term.

To get to the next level: 1) Recognize that you'll have bad days. 2) Focus on progress, not perfection. 3) Calmly renew your mind every time you break your boundaries. 4) Learn to be content with your weight as it is. (This doesn't mean you give up trying to change—just that you become content with the slow process of change.)

Lies you'll need to let go of: I should be changing faster. I shouldn't be breaking my boundaries anymore. It's not worth the effort if I don't see results, and I'm not seeing results. This time is just like all the others. I'll never change anyway, so why bother?

4. BARELY IN CONTROL

In this stage, you're beginning to see some real change in your behavior and even your desires. You still have the occasional bad day and you still think the "eating what you want when you want" life looks pretty attractive. But for the first time, you're thinking, *This really is different than all the other times. I'm changing!* It's exciting.

To get to the next level: 1) Keep renewing your mind. 2) Don't become complacent. 3) Stay in the Word.

Lies you'll need to let go of: I've got this under control now. It's going to be all downhill from here. I don't need to be as diligent with the renewing of the mind now.

5. LIVING IN VICTORY

In this stage, you no longer worry about gaining weight because food no longer controls you. Your weight is constant and doesn't fluctuate more than a few pounds unless you're still losing weight.

To maintain this level: 1) Make a commitment to follow your boundaries faithfully even though you can break them at this point without eating everything in sight. 2) Renew your mind whenever it's necessary to live out your commitment.

Lies you'll need to let go of: In this stage, you don't usually believe any lies. You just have to be careful you don't move into the next stage and watch out for situations that might drive you back into emotional eating. Here's an example: Years ago, I reached the point where I never even *felt* like breaking my boundaries. But then I started to write—and writing made me want to break my boundaries. So I had to learn how to go to God for help with procrastination and all the insecurities writing brought into my life, rather than to food for help.

6. LIVING RECKLESSLY IN VICTORY

I hate to include this stage because I'd just as soon end on a positive note, but I'm afraid it's a real stage. The danger of living in victory is that it's easy to become complacent. Since you know food doesn't control you anymore, it's easy to become lax about the boundaries.

I've had this happen to me on numerous occasions in the last eleven years, but it has never made me gain more than a few pounds. If I start breaking my boundaries too often, I just start renewing my mind again and I'm usually back on track within a few days.

If you haven't reached the living in victory stage yet—and I would be shocked if you had after such a short time—don't get discouraged. Just keep plugging away. You'll get there!

To go back to the last level: 1) Recommit to your boundaries. 2) Renew your mind every time you break them until you're on track again.

Lies you'll need to let go of: I don't need to follow my boundaries anymore because food no longer controls me. Here's the truth: If you love to eat, enjoy eating unhealthy quantities of food, and/or eat for emotional reasons, you will always need boundaries. That's okay, though, because life is better with boundaries!

BIBLE STUDY

1. Glance over the above stages. What stage are you in right now?

2. What will you need to do to get to the next stage?

3. What lies will you need to let go of to get to the next level? Record the truth for each lie and consider reviewing those truths once or twice a day.

4. Review the first lesson in this Bible study and answer the following questions.

   a. Who is the One who moves you from stage to stage?

   b. What is your responsibility in the process?

   c. On a scale of 1 to 10, how diligent have you been with your responsibility?

5. In addition to renewing your mind and abiding in God's Word, what can you do as you wait for God to transform you?

   a. Proverbs 3:5-6

   b. Jeremiah 29:11-13

   c. Philippians 4:11-13

    d. 1 Thessalonians 5:16-18

6. Visit with God about your experiences with weight loss and where you're at right now. Write a prayer below, using Philippians 4:6 as your guide. As you write, try to focus on thanksgiving.

ASSIGNMENT

1. Review your answer to the second question in today's lesson. What is one step you can take today to break free from the control of food?

2. Answer the "I'll Start Tomorrow" questions from page 39 of this study in your journal. Try not to look at the answers you gave last time as God can give you new insights each time you answer these questions.

But There's a Good Reason to Break My Boundaries

THE MORE I work on breaking bad habits, the more I realize how deceitful my mind is. I rarely come right out and say, "I'm going to break my boundaries." Instead, I try to make it seem like I'm *not* really breaking my boundaries. I do that by telling myself little lies. See if any of these lies sound familiar:

- We say, "I don't eat that much," when we're nibbling and sipping high-calorie drinks right and left.

- We say, "I'm hungry," when really, there was just that tiny little twinge in the pit of our stomach, and we're not real sure if it was hunger or just a small twinge.

- We say, "I'm following my boundaries," when really, we're only following them until about 7:00 each night.

- We say, "This is part of my lunch," when really, we just noticed it when we were clearing the table *after* lunch.

So here's my question: Why do we bother lying to ourselves? Why not just tell ourselves the truth? Just say, "You know what? I'm going to break my boundaries. That seems like a good idea."

We lie to ourselves because we know it's *not* a good idea. So we wrack our brains for some way to make it *okay* to eat—either by saying we're not really breaking our boundaries, or by coming up with some reason of why, *in this situation*, it's actually a good idea to break our boundaries, possibly even noble.

53

Can you think of anyone else in the Bible who indulged in this line of thinking? I can. Eve. In the garden. Remember? God told her not to eat the fruit. But by the time Eve was through talking to Satan, it was almost as if she were doing a noble thing by eating it: *This will make me wise. How could that not be helpful?*

We go through the same thinking process with eating. We say, "Of course anyone would eat in this situation. It's a holiday. Or it's free. Or everyone else is eating. It would be unsociable not to eat."

See how we're beginning to slip into the this-is-so-noble-of-me-to-break-my-boundaries mindset? That said, I do think there are times when we need to break our boundaries to love others well.

Here are a few times I would break them: when your 4-year-old brings you breakfast in bed. When someone you don't know very well invites you over for tea and makes homemade lemon bars just for you. When you're visiting a foreign country where it would be rude to not eat.

In some situations, you may need to break your boundaries in order to love well. But those situations are few and far between. Usually, you can plan ahead for occasions like that. If an unexpected occasion comes up, examine your thoughts and ask God for wisdom. Are you justifying the breaking of your boundaries? And if so, is the justification valid? The vast majority of the time, the answer to that question will be *no*.

BIBLE STUDY

1. Do you ever tell yourself any of the lies I mentioned at the beginning of this lesson? If so, which lies?

2. Why do you think you say those things to yourself rather than just telling yourself the truth?

3. What do you think would happen if you started telling yourself the truth each time you wanted to break your boundaries?

4. Read the following phrases and complete them the way you often complete them in real life. You will probably have more than one ending for each phrase.

   a. I'm not really breaking my boundaries. I'm just...

   b. It would be crazy not to break my boundaries in *this* situation because...

5. Write the truth for four of the sentences you just completed above.

   a. Truth:

   b. Truth:

c. Truth:

d. Truth:

6. According to the following Bible verses, what can you do to break free from denial and justification eating?

a. Psalm 120:2

b. 2 Corinthians 10:3-5

c. 1 Thessalonians 5:6

d. 1 Thessalonians 5:21

ASSIGNMENT

1. Be honest about every bite that goes in your mouth today. Try not to eat even one bite or lick of the spoon outside your boundaries.

2. If you had more than four sentences in #4, write the truth for each of the remaining sentences in your journal.

3. Answer the "I'll Start Tomorrow" questions from page 39 in your journal unless you're already saying, "I love having boundaries!"

I Deserve a Donut

*D*O YOU EVER feel like you deserve at least *one* little out-of-the-boundary treat? I do. It's hard to break free from entitlement eating because we hear the message everywhere we go: *You shouldn't have to suffer. You deserve the good life.*

This philosophy encourages us to eat in a couple of different ways. First, we feel we have a right to eat tasty food when it's available. And second, we feel we have a right to live the life we've always dreamed of living. When life fails to live up to our unrealistic expectations for it, we eat to console ourselves. If we can't get the good life, we can at least get a good treat!

Our best—and maybe only—hope for breaking free from entitlement eating is to give up this whole idea of entitlement. We do that by getting a biblical perspective of life. Let's take a look at what Jesus said about life and how we should live it.

BIBLE STUDY

Read Mark 10:35-45 and answer the following questions:

1. What did James and John want? (35-37)

2. Why do you think they wanted that?

3. What did Jesus want James and John to do? (42-44)

4. What kind of life does Jesus want *us* to live? (See also Matthew 22:36-39 and 1 John 3:16-18.)

5. What kind of life does the world tell us to live?

6. What's the difference between the two different lifestyles?

7. What happens when you start feeling like you deserve the good life?

8. It's interesting to see how Jesus responded when James and John asked if they could sit next to Him. He didn't get mad. He didn't get frustrated. He didn't say, "I can't believe how self-centered you guys are." Instead, He just patiently told them what He expected from them as Christians. Why do you think Jesus was so understanding? (Hebrews 4:15, Matthew 4:8-9)

9. Do you think Jesus understands how hard it is to give up the "good life" of eating what you want when you want? Why or why not? (Hebrews 4:15; Matthew 4:3-4)

10. How does it make you feel to know that He understands?

11. What can you do today to break free from I-deserve-a-donut eating?

ASSIGNMENT

1. Review the Bible verses you memorized on Day 5.

2. Try to serve someone sacrificially today.

3. Answer the "I'll Start Tomorrow" questions from page 39 in your journal unless you're already saying, "I love having boundaries!"

Is Skinny Really Necessary?

WHEN I WAS a 9th grader, I tried out for the high school dance team. The team was made up of popular, skinny girls who performed Rockettes-type dance moves at the high school basketball and football games.

I'm not sure why I tried out. I wasn't tall. I wasn't dying to perform at sporting events. And I was more of a smart, good girl rather than a cute, popular girl. But I tried out, anyway—and I made it.

The pressure to be skinny was intense. Before each performance, we had to weigh in. If we made weight, we performed. If we didn't, we had to sit out. At 5'2", my weigh-in weight was 107 pounds. If I was over this weight—even by one pound—I couldn't perform.

You can imagine how this struck terror into the heart of an insecure teenage girl. No one wanted to be the "fat" girl who couldn't perform because she didn't make weight. To avoid that stigma, those of us who were borderline in the weight department got started on some bad habits.

We'd diet like crazy before each weigh-in and then eat like crazy afterwards. We were so happy to be through dieting (and performing in our fat-revealing leotards), that we celebrated by eating everything in sight.

This set up a multitude of eating problems at a young age. In my own life, it led to a 30-year struggle with weight and body image. It affected my self-esteem, my confidence, and even my social life. Too often in college, I hung back in my room, not wanting to go to social events because I felt too fat.

Rather than going to God for help with my problems, I went to the diet section at the local library. Surely I could find a diet to help me with my weight-loss woes.

As it turned out, no, I couldn't. Because even if I found a diet I could actually *stay* on—which was unlikely—I couldn't find a diet that would take away that feeling that I had to be skinny to be acceptable.

Here are a few truths I had to drill into my head to break free from the lies I learned on that dance team:

1. My worth is not determined by a number on the scale.

2. Who I am on the inside is more important than who I am on the outside.

3. I don't need to live up to the expectations of others.

DO YOU REALLY HAVE TO BE SKINNY?

Chances are, you're not on a dance team right now. But you know what I'm talking about. Even now, you probably have some event looming in the future that you want to be skinny for. Here's my question: Will it be the end of the world if you're not skinny for that event?

Sure, a few people may judge you—that's inevitable—but does it really matter? Could you learn to not let those people bother you and just love them anyway? Could you learn to see yourself through God's eyes and not the eyes of a culture that says you have to be skinny to be acceptable? Could you learn to be content with where your weight is at right now?

Here's why I ask: Because God doesn't want you to feel like you have to be skinny to be acceptable. Yes, you'll be slim one day if you continue to renew your mind and break free from the control of food. And God *wants* you to break free from the control of food. But He also wants you to see yourself through His eyes—and He cares more about your character than your appearance.

BIBLE STUDY

1. Do you feel like you *have* to be skinny? Why or why not?

2. What's the worst thing that can happen if you don't lose this weight?

3. Are you willing to accept that if it happens?

4. According to the following Bible verses, why do you not need to worry about a) being overweight, b) having others condemn you for being overweight, or c) failing in your weight loss efforts?

   a. Psalm 27:1-5

   b. Psalm 46:1-2, 7

   c. Romans 8:28

   d. Philippians 1:6

5. According to the following Bible verses, what would be a better option than worry?

   a. Matthew 6:33-34

   b. Philippians 4:6-7

   c. Philippians 4:11-13

ASSIGNMENT

1. If you feel like breaking your boundaries today, answer the "I'll Start Tomorrow" questions from page 39 of this study in your journal.

2. Read the following appearance eating tips from *I Deserve a Donut* and do the suggested activity. If you feel like you have to be skinny to be acceptable, consider doing this exercise once a day for the next week.

APPEARANCE EATING TIPS

Because we live in a culture that is obsessed with appearance and defines beautiful as "skinny," it's easy to think we have to be skinny to be acceptable.

This isn't true. God cares more about our insides than our outsides, and He loves us in our as-is condition. If you're tempted to see yourself through the culture's eyes, here's an activity that will help:

Stand in front of the mirror once a day and say (or shout), "Hollywood has no right to tell me I'm unacceptable when the Living God, King of the Universe, says that I AM acceptable!!"

It sounds a little embarrassing, but it works (although you may want to do it when no one else is home).

Day 12

When You're Not Good Enough

ARA SLAMMED THE book shut and stared blankly out the window. It was her freshman year in college and she was meeting her parents and sister in Hawaii for spring break. Her dad had bought her the book for Christmas, another self-help book. He had said he just wanted to help.

As the plane descended through the wispy clouds, Sara worried. *What would he say this time?* She had gained another 10 pounds since Christmas. And even though she was wearing her most flattering pair of jeans, she knew she would never measure up.

Oh well, she thought as the plane bumped to the pavement, *nothing I can do about it now.* Gathering her things, she trudged up the ramp, hoping to hide behind the crowd until she got closer. *Maybe he won't notice.*

He did. Five minutes into their reunion, he asked the question: "Did you gain more weight?"

Hurt and offended she replied, "A little. But there's nothing I can do about it now, so you might as well accept it."

"Well, we had *better* do something about it," her dad replied.

As if he could.

If only he could. At least then she might be skinny.

67

BIBLE STUDY

1. The sad truth is that we all have stories like this. Unfortunately, not all of our stories are in the past. Do you have anyone in your life right now who is critical of your weight or appearance? If so, answer the following questions with that person in mind:

   a. Why do you think this person is condemning of your weight or appearance? What's behind it?

   b. Is this person an accepting, positive, encouraging person by nature?

   c. Given this person's beliefs, level of maturity, and personality, is it realistic to expect him or her to be positive and supportive of you no matter what you weigh? (Note: I'm not asking if it's right or wrong, I'm asking if it's realistic.)

   d. Is there anything you need to accept about this person?

e. Is God enough to satisfy you, even if this person rejects you?

2. If you're a child of God through faith, how does He see you and feel about you?

a. 1 Samuel 16:7

b. Isaiah 62:4-5

c. Jeremiah 31:3-4

d. Jeremiah 31:20

e. Zephaniah 3:17

f. Luke 12:6-7

g. Romans 3:23; Ephesians 2:8-9

h. Ephesians 2:10

i. 1 Peter 2:9-10

3. If God feels that way about you, does it matter what others think?

4. How is God's view of you different than your own and others' view of you?

5. Will God still love you and accept you if you don't lose weight? (You better say yes on this one!)

6. Do you think He wants you to lose weight? Why or why not? If so, why does He want you to lose and how are His reasons different than your own reasons or the reasons of the condemning people in your life?

7. How would your life change if you were to see yourself through God's eyes rather than the eyes of the condemning people in your life?

8. What can you thank God for as you work through all these issues connected to your weight?

ASSIGNMENT

Grab a cozy blanket, curl up in your favorite chair, and spend five minutes praying through the Bible verses in today's lesson. Most of these verses can also be found in the insecurity section of *I Deserve a Donut,* as well as in a blog post on my blog called "Insecurity Bible Verses." As you pray, picture God doing the things He says He'll do in those verses.

When the Scale Doesn't Cooperate

I DON'T KNOW ABOUT you, but I don't want to wait around on a boring old diet to lose weight at the rate of one pound per week. I want it to be FAST, FUN, and EASY.

So when I step on the scale after being faithful to my boundaries for *one whole week* and see a big fat zero weight loss, I get discouraged.

So discouraged that I head to the kitchen for an out-of-the-boundaries, high-calorie treat. After all, why suffer if I'm not losing weight? This is an example of bad scale eating. I'm eating because the weight isn't coming off as fast as I'd like.

What I want is a miracle. A nice, steep, diagonal line on a weight loss graph, always heading down in a nice, orderly fashion. What's up with the flat line—or even worse—those weeks when I actually *gain* weight?

What's up is probably water weight. Or maybe just my body taking a little break in preparation for a big leap the following week. When I expect the scale to go down every single week—including the weeks I fudge on my boundaries—then I have unrealistic expectations for weight loss.

If I cling to those unrealistic expectations, one of two things will happen: Either I'll get frustrated with my slow progress and quit following my boundaries in a fit of rebellion, or I'll keep following my boundaries, but with the additional weight of a bad attitude. This will make me want to: a) cheat, b) eat to comfort myself, or c) quit unless I get results *soon.*

If I want to keep following my boundaries with a good attitude, I'll need to renew my mind—preferably the minute I step off the scale. Following is a renewing of the mind exercise you can do if you struggle with bad scale eating.

JOURNAL EXERCISE

Think about your expectations for losing weight, following your boundaries, and/or renewing your mind. Then complete the following half-sentences with as many thoughts as you can think of:

1. Losing weight should be...

2. I shouldn't have to...

3. I should be able to...

4. I can't believe...

5. It's not fair that...

When you're through, go back and write the truth for each thought and spend some time talking to God about your struggle. Here are a couple of examples:

EXAMPLE

Belief: I can't believe I stuck to my boundaries all week and didn't lose weight.

Truth: Well, it happened, so I might as well believe it. Weight never goes down in a nice smooth line. If I keep persevering with my boundaries, I'll lose weight eventually.

Or (depending on the week):

Truth: The truth is, I *didn't* stick to my boundaries all week. It felt like I did because of all that suffering, but in reality, I only stuck to them until about 7:00 each night. That nightly out-of-the-boundaries treat was probably enough to keep me from losing any weight this week.

EXAMPLE

Belief: It's not fair that Bob can eat whatever he wants and never gain an ounce and I suffer and suffer and *suffer*, and I still don't lose weight.

Truth: That's just the way life is and God doesn't want me to resent Bob just because he doesn't have a problem with weight. Forgive me, Father. I know Bob has problems that I don't have. Thank you for all Your blessings and thank You for this trial. Please teach me what you want me to learn and help me be thankful for all You've given me rather than resentful of what you haven't.

BIBLE STUDY

1. Sometimes it helps to remember that weight loss is a trial, and in the Bible, trials are good things. According to the following Bible verses, how should you handle the trial of seeing a high number on the scale?

   a. Romans 5:3-5

   b. Romans 8:28

   c. Galatians 6:9

   d. Philippians 4:6

   e. Philippians 4:11-13

2. Why do you think God doesn't perform a miracle and let all of your weight fall off in one fell swoop the minute you start getting serious about your boundaries?

3. Do you think it would be helpful to weigh yourself less often? Why or why not?

4. What can you thank God for today?

ASSIGNMENT

1. If you haven't already done the journal exercise in this lesson, go ahead and do that now.

2. If you're becoming obsessed or discouraged by the scale, you may want to consider weighing yourself less often. If you'd like to make a commitment to weigh yourself less often, record your commitment below. Renew your mind if you break your commitment.

WEIGH-IN COMMITMENT

I will weigh myself _____ times a week.

I won't weigh myself again until _____.

I am getting rid of the scale indefinitely.

Day 14

The Renovation of the Mind

ONE OF THE questions I get asked most frequently is this: How do I renew my mind? We all know we're supposed to do it, but we're not sure *how* to do it. That's not surprising because the renewing of the mind is such a messy process.

In many ways it's similar to a home improvement project: You don't know what you're getting into. You uncover problems you didn't know you had. You have to make multiple calls to your friend the Carpenter for help. And it usually takes longer than you planned. But in the end, the results are so great, you wonder, *Why didn't I do this years ago?*

The renewing of the mind, like a home improvement project, is a taking off and a putting on. You take off the old self. You put on the new self. You take off the lies. You put on the truth. You take off a cultural perspective. You put on a biblical perspective. You take off what you learned growing up. You put on what you learned in the Bible.

Let's see what this looks like in real life. One of the lies you may have learned growing up is that food will make you feel better. Do you remember how you learned that? Let's take a look.

THE BEGINNING OF A LIE

Think back for a minute to your childhood. Did your mom ever sit you down and say, "Honey, whenever you're feeling bad, run as fast as you can to the refrigerator. Don't worry about the consequences. Just eat. It will make you feel better." I'm guessing she didn't.

I bet it was more like this: She gave you a treat to distract you when you had a skinned knee. She said, "Let's have a cup of hot chocolate and some cookies," when the kids made fun of you at school. And she made you a milkshake when you were home sick with the flu and couldn't go to the Valentine's party.

Your mom was just being a wonderful and loving mom. She didn't realize you were picking up lessons along the way, like *Eating will make me feel better,* or *Food is the answer to all of life's problems.*

THE END OF A LIE

It would be nice if we could go back to our moms and have them set us straight: "Honey, I wasn't saying that you should turn to food whenever life is hard. I was just trying to make you feel better." Unfortunately, it will take more than one conversation to unlearn the lies we learned growing up.

We learned those lies situation by situation, and I'm afraid we'll have to unlearn them the same way. Each time we get that urge to eat outside our boundaries, we'll have to renew our minds: Take off the old thoughts. Put on the new thoughts. Take off the lies. Put on the truth. Take off what we learned growing up. Put on what we learned from the Bible.

I Deserve a Donut is a resource you can use to take off lies and put on truth situation by situation. The questions are designed to help you see the lies you're believing, and the Bible verses are chosen to help you put on the truth. For today, let's just get an idea of some of the thoughts we'll have to "take off."

BIBLE STUDY

1. Think of the family you grew up in. What did they believe about life, food, and appearance? List as many things as you can think of.

2. Think of the culture you grew up in. What was its attitude toward life, food, and appearance? List as many things as you can think of.

3. Think of the schools you attended or any significant relationships you've had. Have you learned any lies from them? If so, list them.

4. Now look back through everything you've learned so far. How are those beliefs contributing to your current problem with eating?

5. What do you think would happen if you took off those lies and replaced them with truth?

6. Read Ephesians 4:22-24 and answer the questions that follow:

   That in reference to your former manner of life, you lay aside the old self, which is being corrupted in accordance with the lusts of deceit, and that you be renewed in the spirit of your mind, and put on the new self, which in the likeness of God has been created in righteousness and holiness of the truth.

   a. Think specifically of your goal of breaking free from the control of food. What three things does the passage tell you to do if you want to be transformed?

   b. What is the old self being corrupted by?

   c. Look back at some of the lies (deceit) you learned growing up. In what ways are those lies creating a lust (intense desire) for food?

   d. In what ways are those lies creating a lust for being skinny?

    e. If you take off those lies and replace them with truth, what do you think will happen?

    f. Paul says that the new self is created in righteousness and holiness that comes from the truth. Look back over the lies you wrote down on the previous two pages. Why do you think the truth would make you holy?

7. How would your life change if you were to develop a consistent renewing of the mind habit?

ASSIGNMENT

Look back at the lies you listed in questions 1-3. Over the next few days, record the truth for each lie in your journal. As you write the truth, make a conscious effort to take off the lie you learned growing up and put on the truth that will set you free from the control of food.

Day 15

A Renewing-the-Mind Challenge

*Y*OU'VE SEEN THE headlines: *Lose 20 Pounds in 3 Weeks! Eat All You Want and Lose! 4 Weeks to Your Best Body Ever!!* Combine those headlines with a naïve optimism, and we have a recipe for a lifelong problem with weight.

Why? Because we believe the headlines. We think that losing weight should be fun and easy. So when we find ourselves breaking our boundaries right and left, we don't think, *I need to renew my mind so I have the strength to follow my boundaries.* Instead, we think, *I need to find a new set of boundaries because these boundaries obviously don't work.*

Here's what we're doing: we're trusting in the boundaries. We're believing the lie that somewhere out there is the perfect set of boundaries. And when we find them, they'll be easy to follow.

The sooner we get that lie out of our system the better. We're transformed by the renewing of the mind. Not by the boundaries. And it's not easy to develop a renewing-the-mind habit.

It would be far easier to drown our sorrows in ice cream while poring through a bunch of library books on different diets we might try. But this is one of those times where the good things in life don't come easy.

Nothing is better than sweet fellowship with God. And the renewing of the mind is an opportunity for sweet, sweet fellowship with Him as we take a breather from life's difficulties and look at life from His perspective.

But how do you make yourself take the time to develop the habit? Especially if you're not real great at making yourself do things you don't want to do? Here are six tips that will help you develop a renewing-the-mind habit:

1. Make a plan.

The first step in developing a renewing of the mind habit is to make a plan. How often will you renew your mind? When will you renew your mind? How will you renew your mind? Once you have a plan, you'll be more motivated to work on it.

2. Renew your mind at the same time every day.

When I was struggling with writing, my son gave me some good advice: "Mom, just pick a time to write, and do it at the same time every day. It will get easier as time goes by." He was right—it did get easier. If you're struggling with renewing your mind, try to do it at the same time every day so you develop a habit.

3. Get your ducks in a row.

If you have to search for your Bible, *I Deserve a Donut* book, or journal and pen every time you renew your mind, you won't want to do it. Make it easy by having everything in one place so it's easy to grab.

4. Remember that you have an enemy.

Never forget that you're in a spiritual battle. Satan doesn't want you to renew your mind because he doesn't want you to a) see life from a biblical perspective, b) break free from your strongholds, c) develop a closer walk with God, and d) develop lasting change in your behavior. Especially in the beginning, you'll have to fight opposition to develop this habit.

5. Get an accountability partner.

Sometimes it helps to have a friend hold you accountable to the renewing of your mind. If possible, find a friend to do this study with and hold each other accountable to renewing your mind each day.

6. Renew your mind about the renewing of the mind.

The best way to develop any habit is to set a goal and then renew your mind whenever you don't feel like working on your habit. This is also true with a renewing-the-mind habit. Set a goal (I'll renew my mind every time I break my boundaries, for example) and then renew your mind about the renewing of the mind whenever you don't feel like doing it.

I've included six sets of questions you can use for this purpose, along with some Bible verses, at the back of the book. If you don't feel like renewing your mind, turn to Appendix C, choose a set of questions, and answer the questions in your journal.

If you feel like renewing your mind after you do the questions, fine, do another set of questions for eating. If you don't, don't worry about it. Do the same thing each time you don't feel like renewing your mind, and sooner or later you'll actually *want* to renew your mind.

BIBLE STUDY

1. Do you have a hard time making yourself renew your mind each day? If so, why do you think it's so hard?

2. Look back over today's lesson. Which tips do you think would help you the most to develop a renewing-the-mind habit?

3. According to the following Bible verses, why does God want you to spend time with Him each day? (Note: You can find all of these verses in Appendix C.)

a. Isaiah 62:4-5

b. Jeremiah 29:13

c. Jeremiah 31:3-4

d. John 15:4

e. Romans 12:2

f. Galatians 5:16

g. Hebrews 12:11

4. In summary, what are the benefits of renewing your mind and spending time with God in His Word and prayer?

RENEWING OF THE MIND CHALLENGE

Consider making a commitment to renew your mind by accepting one of the challenges below. I would encourage you to go for #2, #3, or #4 as those will be the most helpful. I broke free from the control of food with challenge #2, although I could have done it faster with one of the other challenges!

1. **The get-your-feet-wet-challenge:** Renew your mind once a day. The easiest way to renew your mind is to choose a set of questions from *I Deserve a Donut* and write the answers in your journal or pray through the Bible verses.

2. **The middle-of-the-road challenge:** Renew your mind whenever you break your boundaries, preferably before you eat another bite.

3. **The hardcore challenge:** Renew your mind once a day plus whenever you break your boundaries.

4. **The harder-than-hardcore challenge:** Renew your mind once or twice a day plus whenever you *feel* like breaking your boundaries. (Note: I could never get myself to do this challenge because I always wanted to eat too much, but if you can make yourself do it, this is definitely more efficient in the weight loss department.)

I will commit to the _____ challenge.

ASSIGNMENT

Read "How to Use This Book" (or "How to Use This App" in the "Other Resources" section) in *I Deserve a Donut* if you haven't already read it. Then choose a set of questions from the book (or app) and answer them in your journal.

Whenever you have the time, try to answer the questions in your journal, rather than in your head. This serves several purposes. First, it will make you less likely to break your boundaries if you know you have to take the time to write out the answers.

Second, studies have shown that the more senses you involve in the learning process, the better you learn. So thinking *and* writing will help you learn the truth at a deeper level than just thinking.

Finally, I've found that I answer the questions more fully when I take the time to write out the answers. It seems like God pours more truth in when I write, but maybe that's just because I'm spending more time listening when I write.

Day 16

I Might As Well Eat

*P*ICTURE THIS: YOU'RE clearing the table after dinner, and you can't get your mind off the brownie you just ate for dessert. It was *so* good. And there are more brownies just sitting there, all alone on the counter, just waiting to be eaten.

Maybe you could have just one little bite. What would that hurt? You reach for a knife and cut off a tiny piece. *Mmmm,* just as good as you remembered. You set down the knife and go back to washing dishes.

But that brownie is still calling your name. It's distracting. How about just one more teensy bite? After all, you've already broken your boundaries. What could one more bite hurt?

We all know what happens next, right? Before you know it, you've not only finished off the whole brownie but also a few more.

This is an example of failure eating. When we break our boundaries, even by one bite, we feel like a failure. And when we feel like a failure, we eat. By far the best way to break free from failure eating is to reach for the questions and Bible verses in *I Deserve a Donut* instead of the next bite.

There's just one problem. Sometimes we want that brownie so much we can't make ourselves do the questions or the verses. That used to happen to me all the time, so here's what I did: I ate the brownie. Then I renewed my mind. Not very efficient in the weight-loss department, but at least it helped me avoid an all-out binge.

If you want to be more efficient than I was, try making a

89

bargain with yourself: You can have another brownie—in fact, you're *going* to have another brownie—but you have to write out the answers to a set of questions in *I Deserve a Donut* first. Nine times out of ten, when I use this approach, I don't want another brownie by the time I finish with the questions.

If you can't make yourself use this approach, don't beat yourself up. Just renew your mind as soon as possible after you break your boundaries—preferably before you eat another bite.

BIBLE STUDY

1. One of the things I love about the Bible is that we get to see how Jesus handled temptation. Since we're trying to say no to temptation ourselves, what could be better than to see what Jesus did? Read Luke 4:1-13 and record everything you see about how Jesus responded to temptation.

2. It's easy to brush off this section of Scripture and think, *Oh yeah, Jesus was tempted, but He was God. How bad could it have been?* The truth is, it was bad. The experience was so grueling that the angels had to come and minister to Jesus when it was over (Matthew 4:11). One of our temptations is to make life about food. Read Luke 4:3-9. What were Jesus's temptations?

3. Read the passage again. Was it always obvious that Satan was asking Jesus to do something against God's will? Explain.

Satan is the master of the partial truth. His lies look so much like truth that we think *of course* we should break our boundaries in *this* situation. That's why it's so important to carry our thoughts captive to the truth when we're tempted. We can and should ask God to help us, but that should always go hand in hand with using the help He's already given us—the Bible.

1. Why do you think Jesus quoted Bible verses rather than just asking God to help Him say no to temptation?

2. What do you usually do when you're tempted to break your boundaries?

3. What do you think would happen if you took the time to pray through or meditate on some Bible verses every time you were tempted?

ASSIGNMENT

Review the Bible verses you memorized on Day 5 of this study by trying to write them from memory in your journal. If you're tempted to break your boundaries today, pull out those Bible verses and use them to say no to temptation.

I'll Never Change

AVE YOU EVER thought, *I'll never get over this. I'll be struggling with weight 'til the day I die?* I used to think that. What I came to realize through hours of truth journaling is that the battle wasn't hopeless as long as I kept fighting lies with truth. God used the truth to set me free. But before He set me free, He gave me hope.

After an evening of breaking my boundaries, I'd write in my journal: *This time is just like all the others. I'll never change.* Then God would answer: *This time isn't like all the others—because this time you're fighting lies with truth. And the truth will set you free.*

He was right. But in order to break free, I had to keep renewing my mind—even when I was sick to death of renewing my mind.

I know how hard it is to persevere with this struggle. It would be nice if God would just change us instantly. Unfortunately, He doesn't usually do that. Instead, He wants us to get involved in our own healing. Today's Bible study is about another man who was asked to get involved in his own healing. Let's see what we can learn from his example.

BIBLE STUDY

1. Read 2 Kings 5:1-6. What was Naaman's goal?

2. What is your goal with this study?

3. Read 2 Kings 5:7-9. What do you think Naaman was expecting as he stood at the door waiting for Elisha to come?

4. Read 2 Kings 5:10. How would you feel if some guy you didn't even know came to the door and told you that you had to jump in the river seven times if you wanted to be healed?

5. Think of your own goal of losing weight and breaking free from the control of food. What were you expecting as you began this study? Were you expecting it to be the somewhat easy answer to losing weight and keeping it off? If so, how are you feeling now?

6. Read 2 Kings 5:11-12. Why do you think Naaman responded this way to Elisha's instructions?

7. How do you respond when you don't lose weight as quickly as you'd like?

8. God could have healed Naaman instantly. Why do you think He didn't?

9. Why do you think God hasn't given you instant success in the area of weight loss?

10. Read 2 Kings 5:13-15. Did God eventually heal Naaman? What did Naaman learn through this experience?

11. Sometimes we forget that God loves us and uses our trials to teach us. Can you think of any lessons God might want you to learn through the trial of losing weight?

12. Do you think God would have healed Naaman if he had given up after the 4th dip? Why or why not?

13. Read Romans 12:2 and John 15:4-5. Do you think God will transform you if you don't make the effort to renew your mind and to abide in Him and His Word? Why or why not?

14. What was Naaman's role in the healing process? What was God's role?

15. Review the first lesson in this book. What is your role in the "breaking free from the control of food" process? What is God's role?

16. How are you doing with your role?

If you're not doing well with your role, please don't beat yourself up or get discouraged. This is a journey, not an "I have to do this right now or it will be my last chance" effort. Just do what you can and keep pressing on.

ASSIGNMENT

Have a little visit with God about your food issues and your experiences with the renewing of the mind. As you're visiting with Him, remember that He loves you and wants to help you.

Day 18

Is Overeating a Sin? Part One

OFTEN WITH A bad habit, I know I should set some boundaries, but the habit never seems bad enough to make a real commitment to it. So I stumble through life with the thought always in the back of my mind, *I should really do something about that habit*, but I never get around to it.

Unless I'm convicted that I *need* to change, I don't change. I'm much more willing to commit to boundaries if I see that my habit is a sin. So today and tomorrow I want to look at three questions we can ask ourselves to determine if our habit of overeating has stepped over into the sin category. We'll do one question today and two tomorrow. Here's the first question.

ARE YOU TURNING TO FOOD
TO COPE WITH LIFE?

One of the wonderful things about God is that He uses our trials to draw us closer to Him and make us more like Him. It's a brilliant plan. He gives us the gift of free will, even though He knows we'll sometimes use our free will to do things He doesn't want us to do.

This results in trials. But when He sees us suffering from those trials, He doesn't say, "Well, look at them, I knew that would happen. They're so stupid." No, instead He steps in and redeems our trials by using them for our good. He is a loving, compassionate, gracious, and wise Father—and He wants to help us with our problems.

So why do we say, "No, I think I'd rather go get something to eat"? Crazy. We think this is a harmless activity—in fact, we even joke about drowning our sorrows in ice cream—but the truth is, it's dangerous.

Why? Because we're developing a habit of going to food for help with life's problems. Not only is that unwise—since food can't solve our problems—but it also puts us at risk for making an idol of food.

That may sound drastic but listen to this description of a man with his idol in Isaiah 44:17: "He falls down before it and worships; he also prays to it and says, 'Deliver me, for you are my god.'"

Doesn't that sound like us with our favorite treats? First, we do a little worship talk: *Oh, this is so great!!* Then, we turn to it for deliverance: *Ahh, a little chocolate will make me feel better.*

We're 21st century people so we're not going to bow down before our bowl of ice cream and say, "Deliver me, for you are my god." That would be ridiculous. But don't we do that in practice even though we don't say the words?

1. Why do you suppose the Israelites turned to their idols for deliverance when their idols were obviously powerless to help them?

2. Why do you suppose we turn to food for deliverance when it is obviously powerless to help us?

3. When we consistently turn to food for help with life's problems, not only are we turning food into an idol (Philippians 3:18-19), we're also missing out on all that God wants to give us. According to the following verses, what will God do for us if we go to Him for help with our problems?

a. Psalm 46:1-2

b. Hebrews 12:7-11

c. Galatians 5:16, 22-23

4. What do you get when you turn to food for help with life?

5. Who is the better helper?

ASSIGNMENT

What is the biggest trial you're going through right now? What emotion are you experiencing with that trial? Turn to that emotion in *I Deserve a Donut* and use the questions and/ or Bible verses to go to God rather than food for help with your trial. You can also find many of these Bible verses and questions on my blog under the "Live in Peace" tab.

Day 19

Is Overeating a Sin? Part Two

IN LUKE 10:27 Jesus tells us to love God with all our heart, soul, mind, and strength. It stands to reason then that anything that gets in the way of that is a sin. Today we'll look at two more questions we can ask ourselves to see if overeating has stepped into the sin category for us.

ARE YOU LUSTING AFTER FOOD?

Do you ever have days when you want to eat everything in sight, and when that's gone, go out and eat some more? Those are the days we're lusting after food. The meaning of lust is "intense desire." It's not a "Yes, this is great, but I can take it or leave it" feeling. It's an all out "I have to have it!" sensation.

1. The problem with lust is that it interferes with our relationship with God. Think of it this way. How would you feel if you were married and your spouse was obsessed with some other person or thing?

2. How do you think God feels when we're obsessed with some other person or thing?

God *loves* us. He wants us to be satisfied with Him alone—but lust distracts us. It shouts, "God isn't enough! You need more! Go get it!!!" When we answer its voice, we never get enough to fill us up (Jeremiah 2:13). Our souls are in a constant state of turmoil (1 Peter 2:11). Because we were created to worship God, He is the *only* One who can satisfy us.

3. Think of those days when all you want to do is eat. What is life like on those days?

4. Now think of some of your best moments or days with God. What is life like on those days?

5. Which days are better?

6. One of the best ways to avoid lust is to maintain strict boundaries. Why do you think that is? (See also Romans 13:14.)

If you're already in a full-blown lust situation, here are a few things you can do to break out of it:

1. Have a list of Bible verses at hand to pray through whenever the lust hits.

2. Think of all the things you're clinging to, then mentally give them up to God one at a time. That doesn't mean you have to physically give them up (you still have to eat, for example), just let go of your demanding spirit.

3. Answer the greed/lust questions from *I Deserve a Donut*, preferably in your journal.

4. Have a conversation with God about all the Bible verses in the greed/lust section of *I Deserve a Donut*.

5. Follow Paul's advice in Philippians 4:6-7 and pray with thanksgiving. Make your request to God and then start thanking Him for everything you can think of to thank Him for. Keep thanking Him until you start feeling content.

ARE YOU WILLING TO SET BOUNDARIES, IF NECESSARY?

Loving God with all our heart, soul, mind, and strength implies a willingness to give up everything else to follow Him (Mark 10:17-27). An unwillingness to set boundaries could be a sign that we're not willing to give everything up.

What we're unwilling to give up varies. It might be food. It might be freedom. It might be comfort. Or it might just be our "rights"—the right to eat what we want when we want.

7. What do you have the hardest time giving up? Is it the food itself, or is it something else (comfort, excitement, your rights, etc.)?

8. If you aren't willing to set boundaries, do you think that's a sign that you're not willing to give up everything for God or is that over-spiritualizing boundaries in eating? Explain.

ASSIGNMENT

Look back at the suggestions I gave for breaking free from lust in today's lesson. Try one of those suggestions.

Day 20

How Are You Doing?

SOMETIMES IT HELPS to take a break and look at life. Find out what's working, what's not, and what needs to change. It also helps do that with eating. Since we're more than halfway through the study, I thought it would be nice to take a break and do a little evaluation. As you answer the questions, try to discover your areas of weakness and what you can do to help.

For example, I discovered that one of my biggest problems was late afternoon eating. Just knowing it's a problem will help me watch out for it. But I could also make a plan to have another quiet time or do a set of questions every day at 3:00. This would help me prepare mentally for the coming temptation. Go ahead and answer the questions to see if there's anything you can do to help with your own areas of weakness.

1. What are your boundaries?

2. What time of the day or week are you most likely to break your boundaries?

3. Why do you think you often break them at that time?

4. What situations cause you to break your boundaries (for example, bad days, eating out, transitions, etc.)?

5. Are you going through a trial right now that's making you want to eat? Explain.

6. Do you eat for any of the following emotions? Circle any that apply: anger, worry, boredom, stress, discontentment, insecurity, self-condemnation, frustration.

7. Look at your answers to the last five questions. Can you think of any practical things you can do to make it easier to follow your boundaries? Brainstorm a list. Here are some examples: Go through one set of donut questions after dinner each night. Have your housemates hide your favorite foods from you (I've done this). Pray through Bible verses while you're waiting for your coffee to heat up each morning. List any ideas you have.

8. Although it's helpful to establish practical boundaries, if we want lasting change, we'll need to renew our minds (Romans 12:2). On a scale of 1 to 10, how diligent have you been with renewing your mind?

9. If you haven't been very diligent, what's getting in the way?

10. Can you think of any practical things you can do to make it easier to renew your mind?

SECONDARY BOUNDARIES

If you find yourself constantly breaking your boundaries, it may be helpful to establish secondary boundaries. Primary boundaries are your main boundaries: three meals a day, hunger only, 30 points a day, etc. Secondary boundaries are boundaries you put in place to make it easier to follow your primary boundaries. Here's how you come up with them: Take a look at your failures.

For example, if I have sweets for breakfast, I almost always break my boundaries later in the day. Since this is an area of repeated failure, I've made a secondary boundary: no sweets before lunch. Here are some secondary boundaries others have added:

- Sweets for social occasions only.
- No eating in front of the television or while reading.
- No eating while standing or driving.

- No second helpings (I also have this boundary).

- No eating after 7:00 p.m.

These are just ideas. Find the secondary boundaries that work best for you but don't go overboard with too many.

If you find yourself consistently breaking your boundaries with a particular food and you think it would be easier to eliminate that food rather than eat it in limited amounts, do that. You can always bring it back into your life later.

Always remember—the boundaries aren't magical. No matter what boundaries you choose, they will be hard to follow. The key to breaking free from the control of food is to renew your mind. Boundaries simply tell you *when* you need to renew your mind.

ASSIGNMENT

1. Look over your answers to the questions above. Would it be helpful to add any secondary boundaries? If so, choose one or two secondary boundaries to add to your primary boundaries. Don't set too many or it will overwhelm you.

2. Write your secondary boundaries on index cards and post them in the kitchen so you'll remember them.

3. Try not to eat even one bite outside of your boundaries today, including your secondary boundaries.

Day 21

I. Need. Chocolate.

EGAN STILL REMEMBERS the first time she ate for emotional reasons. She had been asked out on a date by a nice Christian boy and was eagerly anticipating it. That is, until her friend heard about it.

"Ryan?" her friend said, "He's a jerk. He says he's a Christian, but he sure doesn't act it. He'll be all over you on your date."

Megan didn't know what to do. She was too embarrassed to cancel the date so she went through with it. Her friend was right. She spent the whole night fending off Ryan's advances. She was so relieved when it was over that she made a big bowl of hot, buttered popcorn and sat in front of the television recovering.

This started a career in emotional eating that isn't over to this day, even though Megan is now married with a couple of kids. Megan's story isn't unique. Most of us begin emotional eating at a young age. That's one of the reasons it's so hard to overcome. It's almost like we're giving up a friend.

There are two ways to break free from emotional eating. First, you can learn not to eat when you're emotional. Second, you can learn to let go of the emotion. If you get rid of the emotion, you get rid of the desire to eat.

Let's see how each approach would have worked in Megan's situation. If she had used the first strategy, she would have come home from the date and answered the emotional eating questions on page 31 of *I Deserve a Donut*. These would have helped her see

107

that popcorn wasn't going to solve her problems and that it would be better to eat with control.

If she had used the second strategy, she would have come home and asked herself, "What emotion am I experiencing?" and then flipped to those questions and Bible verses in *I Deserve a Donut*. Let's see what that would have looked like.

Put yourself in her place for a minute. You're a teenage girl who just came home from a very stressful first date. How would you be feeling? Would you be annoyed with the boy? Would you be worried about what he was going to tell the kids at school? Would you be feeling bad for telling him no? Would you be worried that all boys were like this? Or would you be kicking yourself for accepting the date in the first place?

The truth is, we would all respond differently depending on our personalities and previous experiences in life. And it would be wonderful to talk to God about our responses. The anger, insecurity, worry, or regret questions from *I Deserve a Donut* would help us discuss the situation with God and look at it from *His* perspective. Do you see how helpful that would be? Not just in terms of weight loss, but for overall help with life?

When we stuff our emotions with food, we miss out on so much. We can change that by developing a habit of going to God to talk through all those hard situations in our lives that make us want to eat for emotional reasons. Let's give that a try with today's Bible study.

BIBLE STUDY

1. List some of the hard things going on in your life right now that make you feel like overeating. Choose one of those trials to focus on for today's study.

2. Read Hebrews 12:1-15 and record everything it says about how God wants you to handle this trial and what He's hoping you'll get out of it. Try to make it personal. For example, in verse 1, what does He want *you* to lay aside?

3. How are you currently responding to this trial?

4. What will happen if you keep doing what you've been doing with this trial?

5. What do you need to change to handle your trial the way God wants you to handle it?

6. Read James 1:2-4 and Romans 5:3-5. What do you think God wants to teach you through this trial that you're going through? Be specific.

7. When you think of all God could do in your life through this trial, can you see why the trial could be a good thing in your life?

8. What will you need to do if you want to accomplish God's goals for your trial? (Romans 12:1-2; Hebrews 12:11)

ASSIGNMENT

1. Try to be aware of your emotions today. If you get the sudden urge to eat outside of your boundaries, ask yourself, "What just happened that made me want to eat?"

2. Go to God for help by journaling through one set of questions or praying through one set of Bible verses in the "Emotions That Make You Eat" section of *I Deserve a Donut*. You can also find some of these questions and Bible verses under the "Live in Peace" tab at my blog.

Day 22

Breaking Free from Binges

INGEING IS PROBABLY the most demoralizing behavior in our eating repertoire. Not only do we face a possible weight gain, but most of the time we don't even enjoy the eating session. Instead, we go directly from *I can't get enough* to *I wish I hadn't eaten so much*. Then we finish the evening off with *I'm a total failure* and *I'll never get over this*.

By far the absolute best way to avoid a binge is to renew your mind as soon as you break your boundaries, especially at night if that's when you normally binge. If you can't make yourself do that, renew your mind after the episode is over, preferably before you go to bed. The hopeless, failure, regret, and self-condemnation questions and Bible verses in *I Deserve a Donut* are all helpful in a post-binge situation.

When you wake up the morning after the binge, resist the urge to say, "I'm going to stick to my boundaries today!!" This sounds good and hopeful, but the truth is, we're powerless to make ourselves follow our boundaries. We need to constantly rely on God if we want to have hope.

So instead, wake up and spend time with Him. Read your Bible. Do some of the questions. Pray through the Bible verses. Keep doing that as often as possible throughout the day so you have the strength to make it through without another binge.

For our Bible study today, I'm including some of the hopeless eating questions from *I Deserve a Donut* because I think it's good to

111

remember that it is God who will change us through the renewing of the mind, not us through self-control. This always gives me hope when I feel like I'll never break free from whatever habit is controlling me at the moment. *I may be weak, but He is strong.*

BIBLE STUDY

1. How many years have you been struggling with eating too much?

2. How many years (or weeks) have you been diligent about applying truth to the lies that are fueling your habit?

3. On a scale of 1 to 10, how diligent have you been?

4. When you think of how long you've been renewing your mind compared to how long you've been overeating, is it realistic to expect 100% victory at this point? Why or why not?

5. How does God feel about you in the midst of a binge? (Jeremiah 31:3, 20; Hebrews 4:15-16; Romans 8:1)

6. What would He like to do for you?

    a. Psalm 3:3-5

    b. Psalm 91:2-4

    c. Philippians 1:6

7. What would He like you to do?

    a. John 8:10-11

    b. John 15:4

    c. Romans 12:1-2

    d. Galatians 6:9

e. James 1:16-17

8. What will you gain if you do what He wants you to do?

9. What sacrifices will you have to make to do what He wants you to do?

10. When you think of what you'll gain, is it worth the sacrifice?

ASSIGNMENT

Think of the day ahead. When will you be most tempted to break your boundaries or binge? Renew your mind by doing a set of questions or having another quiet time right before that situation comes up. For example, if you usually binge in the evening, renew your mind or have a quiet time right after dinner.

Day 23

Spiritual Battle

*L*AST WEEK I was excited about writing because I had come up with this brilliant new system: Write for two hours, take a mandatory one-hour break, then write for another two hours. I was convinced that this would be the answer to all my writing woes because it worked so perfectly the first two days I tried it.

I was wrong. By the third day, I was breaking my boundaries right and left and even going into "time-wasting binge" mode where I'd surf the Internet for an hour or two just to avoid writing. It reminded me of the old days when I used to binge on food. I was out of control.

You would think—since I write books on the renewing of the mind—that I would respond to my failure by renewing my mind. If you thought that, you would be wrong. I responded by being frustrated and thinking my boundaries didn't work.

Here's what I should have done and, thankfully, what I did do this morning: I engaged in spiritual warfare. I pulled out my procrastination Bible verses and had a long conversation with God before I even attempted to write. Those Bible verses and that conversation with God gave me the strength to follow my writing boundaries this morning.

Spiritual warfare is essential if we want to be victorious over our habits. Listen to what Peter tells us in 1 Peter 5:8: "Be of sober spirit. Be on the alert. Your adversary, the devil, prowls around like a roaring lion, seeking someone to devour."

It may seem a little crazy to think Satan cares about procrastination and weight loss. But the truth is, Satan is interested in any activity that controls us, discourages us, and messes us up our lives. He'd like nothing better than to see us controlled by our bad habits for the rest of our lives.

In any battle, it's helpful to know the enemy. Let's spend some time doing that in today's Bible study.

BIBLE STUDY

Read the Bible verses below, and for each passage, answer the following questions: a) What does Satan do to get people to disobey God? b) What might Satan do to get you to give up the struggle and go back to eating what-you-want-when-you-want? c) What will you need to do to withstand temptation? I've done the first one for you.

1. Genesis 3:1-6

   a. He gets Eve to question God and ignore the consequences of disobeying God. He also makes sin look attractive.

   b. He'll try to get me to ignore the consequences of breaking my boundaries and focus on how fun it would be to break them.

   c. I'll need to focus on the consequences of breaking my boundaries and not the benefits!

2. Luke 4:13

3. John 8:44

4. Revelation 12:9-10

According to the following Bible passages, what should you do if you want to stand firm against Satan's attacks?

1. 2 Corinthians 10:3-5

2. Luke 4:1-12

3. Ephesians 6:11-18

4. 1 Peter 5:8

Think of Eve in the Garden of Eden. Why do you think she gave in to temptation?

What will you need to do if you want to avoid giving in to temptation?

ASSIGNMENT

Think of the day ahead. When will you be most tempted to break your boundaries? Engage in spiritual warfare by praying through some Bible verses before temptation hits.

Truth Journaling

I'VE ALWAYS ENJOYED journaling. But it wasn't until I was forty years old that God began to change my life with it. That was the year I started truth journaling.

It began as a marriage improvement exercise. My husband and I were in a Bible study, and we all decided to choose a fault to work on—something that would improve our marriages. I decided to work on my critical spirit.

My plan was to *think positive*. Each time I was critical of my husband, I would write it down and then put a positive thought next to it. I couldn't wait to get started. I bought a journal and began writing down thoughts.

The journal was pretty. The thoughts were not. Some days they were so horrible, I tore the pages from my journal, crumpled them up, and hid them in the garbage can beneath the coffee grounds and banana peels. But I kept writing.

After only a week or two of journaling, I began to notice a pattern. Those ugly thoughts? They were more than ugly. They were lies. And when I replaced the lies with truth, I felt better—about my husband, about my marriage, and about life in general.

Before long, I gave up the *think positive* project and started replacing lies with truth. I called it truth journaling.

I've been truth journaling for twelve years now, and God has used it to transform my life in ways I never thought possible. Truth journaling has done more for my walk with God than any other discipline besides Bible study, as it has become a way to talk through my problems with Him.

I wrote about truth journaling at length in *Freedom from Emotional Eating*, but I'd like to include it in this study as well since it is such a helpful renewing-the-mind tool.

CARRYING THOUGHTS CAPTIVE

Often people advocate the use of journaling as a way to clear the air. To get all those bad thoughts out of our system so they don't poison us. Truth journaling is different. You're still spilling out your thoughts, but for the purpose of examining them and bringing them captive to the truth.

It's a practical application of 2 Corinthians 10:3-5: "For though we walk in the flesh, we do not war according to the flesh, for the weapons of our warfare are not of the flesh but divinely powerful for the destruction of fortresses. We are destroying speculations and every lofty thing raised up against the knowledge of God, and we are taking every thought captive to the obedience of Christ."

The best way to learn how to truth journal is to just jump in and give it a try. Picture yourself in this situation: Your house is a mess, you have a million things to do, and the day ahead looks dreary. You *should* be working on your to-do list, but what you really want to do is break your boundaries and have a bowl of ice cream. Let's try truth journaling.

STEP ONE: SPILL OUT YOUR THOUGHTS

Begin by spilling your thoughts onto the pages of your journal. This usually takes less than a minute. You may end up with six or seven sentences. These aren't "Let's see, what am I thinking?" sorts of thoughts. They're gut level thoughts. In fact, you may even know they're untrue as you write them. Here's what I would write in my journal for the above example:

> My life is a wreck. I'll never be able to get anything done. I'm such a loser. I can't believe I put everything off for so long. I think I'll have some ice cream. That will make me feel better.

Can you see what a jumble my thoughts are? I'm not organizing them first. I'm just spilling them out onto the paper. It took me about 30 seconds.

STEP TWO: NUMBER YOUR THOUGHTS

The next step is to number each sentence. This will force you to look at each thought, rather than the whole overwhelming situation. This isn't natural. Our tendency is to let all those unhealthy thoughts swirl around inside our heads all day. Not only does this stress us and depress us, it also keeps us from taking action. God wants us to actively address these thoughts because they have the power to paralyze us.

Paul's advice—to take each *thought* captive—is brilliant. This allows us to slow down, separate the swirling thoughts, and look at them individually to see how they stack up against truth.

Think of each sentence in your journal as a thought. If it's a long sentence, you may want to break it into a couple of thoughts. In my journal, I put a little number with a circle around it in front of each sentence. Here's what our journal entry would look like after numbering our thoughts:

> 1. My life is a wreck. 2. I'll never be able to get anything done. 3. I'm such a loser. 4. I can't believe I put everything off for so long. 5. I think I'll eat some ice cream. 6. That will make me feel better.

STEP THREE: WRITE THE TRUTH FOR EACH LIE

Next, we'll look at each sentence to see if it's true or false. If it's true, we'll write true. If it's false—or only half-true—we'll rewrite it so it's all the way true.

This step is difficult for a couple of reasons. First, it can take some hard thinking to come up with the truth. Second, we don't always recognize lies when we see them. Sometimes we've believed lies for so long that they look like truth. I usually start out fully believing everything I write down in my journal. It's not until I look at the sentences one at a time that I start thinking, *Hmm, maybe that's not true after all.*

That's why it's so important to bring each *thought* captive. It's easier to spot the lie in one sentence than it is to identify a lie in the whole paragraph. So close your mind to the rest of the paragraph and just focus on that one particular sentence.

For example, if I consider the sentence "My life is a wreck" in light of the rest of the paragraph, I would say, "Yes, my life *is* a wreck. Look at how inept I am." But if I consider that sentence all by itself, I can see the truth: *My life isn't a wreck at all. In fact, it's a pretty good life, overall.*

If you have a hard time knowing if a thought is true, picture Jesus standing in front of you. Would He say, "Barb, your life is a wreck"? No, He wouldn't. He would say, "Barb, your life is a gift. You have so many things to be thankful for." And then He might point out a few things.

Let me show you how I would truth journal the example we just looked at. To make it easier to follow, I'll record the truth after each sentence.

TRUTH JOURNALING

1. My life is a wreck.

Truth: My life is not a wreck. Yes, it's not perfect. But it's not a wreck either. I have a wonderful God, a wonderful family, a wonderful ministry, and I live in a wonderful place. I am blessed.

2. I'll never be able to get anything done.

Truth: God is changing me, and I can do all things through Him who strengthens me. He'll help me get things done when they need to get done. I don't need to worry. His grace is sufficient for me.

3. I'm such a loser.

Truth: I'm not a loser. I'm a delightful child of God. His beloved. His bride. His workmanship. He exults over me with love. He loves me as I am. He doesn't require me to be perfect in order for Him to love me.

4. I can't believe I put everything off for so long.

Truth: I don't know why I can't believe it since I often put things off for this long!

5. I think I'll eat some ice cream.

Truth: I think not! That would be crazy. If I eat ice cream this early in the

morning, I'll be eating all day. It would be far better to wait and have a bowl this evening.

6. That will make me feel better.

Truth: For about FIVE MINUTES!!!! I will be much better off if I just GET TO WORK and start getting things done. Think how good I will feel! I think I'll start right now.

THOUGHTS ON TRUTH JOURNALING

Do you see how truth journaling would make me actually want to say no to the ice cream and get started on my to-do list? Truth journaling can be used for eating and procrastination, but it can also be used to let go of negative emotions.

I still remember the day my two teenage daughters came home steaming mad about something that happened at youth group. They walked in the door, said, "We need to truth journal!!!" and went straight to their rooms to do that. Ten minutes later they walked out like a breath of fresh air, no longer upset about what went on at youth group.

I have seen that same situation play out not only in my own life but also in the lives of countless other women. As we renew our minds, God changes us.

PRACTICE SESSION

For today's study, I'd like to walk you through a truth journaling session so you can give it a try if you're unfamiliar with this tool. Begin by listing three different trials going on in your life right now. They could be hard trials or easy trials.

1.

2.

3.

Choose one of the trials to truth journal about and answer the following questions:

1. What is your trial?

2. What emotion are you experiencing with your trial?

3. Now let's try truth journaling. Read Step One in today's lesson and spill out your thoughts. Don't analyze them. Just write down the first thing that comes to your mind in the space below.

4. Now read Step Two, then go back and number each sentence. If it's a long sentence that contains two thoughts, give each thought a number.

5. Read Step Three and write the truth for each sentence in #3. This is the time to take off your perfectionist hat if you're a perfectionist and just do your best.

6. What did you learn from this experience?

ASSIGNMENT

Try to truth journal one more time before the day is over. If you can't make yourself do it, try going through one set of questions in Appendix C. If you'd like more help with truth journaling, including a video on how to truth journal, look under the renew your mind/renewing of the mind tools tab at barbraveling.com.

TRUTH JOURNALING ATTEMPT #2

Situation:

Emotion:

Thoughts:

Truths:

Day 25

Scripture Prayer

I FIRST READ ABOUT Scripture prayer in Beth Moore's book *Praying God's Word*. Praying Scripture is a powerful way to renew your mind. Here's why: It helps us look at life from God's perspective.

This doesn't always happen with our normal prayers. Often, we spend all of our time telling God what we want and never get around to asking Him what He wants. Here's an example. Let's say I want to lose weight, so I go to God to ask Him to help me. Listen to what a typical prayer might sound like:

> Lord, please help me lose weight. I've been struggling with this for so many years. I'm so tired of the struggle. Joan can eat whatever she wants and not gain a pound. I merely look at a piece of pie and I gain weight. That seems so unfair, God. Couldn't you make me more like Joan? Or at least help me stick to my boundaries? I'm so tired of this. I just want to eat. Help me lose weight, Lord.

Do you think that prayer would help me remember that life is about God and that I should be thankful in all things? Probably not, right? Instead, the prayer just rehearsed my belief that I have a pretty bad life and Joan has a pretty great life. All because she's skinny and I'm not.

CHANGING OUR PERSPECTIVE

Scripture prayers are much more helpful. With Scripture prayers, we're honest with God about our thoughts and feelings but we're also exposing them to the truth of His Word. Here is what a prayer based on Scripture might look like:

> Lord, did you see what I did today? Broke my boundaries again. It's so tiresome, Lord, because I do it all the time. Yet you tell me to rejoice in my trials (James 1:2-4). This is a trial. What do you want me to learn from it, Lord? (I would take a break to listen here.)
>
> I'm guessing you might want me to learn not to care so much about being skinny, or maybe to be content and not so envious of Joan. Could you also teach me to follow my boundaries?
>
> You say that I'll reap if I don't grow weary. Thank you for that. You say I have need of endurance. Help me endure. By You I can run upon a troop and leap over a wall! You will change me, Lord. Thank you! (Galatians 6:9; Hebrews 10:36; Psalm 18:29)
>
> It helps to know that you understand what I'm going through. You've been tempted yourself. You are a wonderful God, a dear Creator, my beloved Savior. Thank you for all you've done and all you'll continue to do. Weeping may last for a night, but a shout of joy comes in the morning. I'm already shouting, Lord. Praise your holy Name! (Hebrews 4:15-16; Hebrews 12:11; Psalm 30:5)

Do you see how much more helpful this prayer is than my first prayer? The Bible verses I used are from the hopeless eating section of *I Deserve a Donut*. If you haven't tried praying Scripture yet, I hope you'll give it a try. Just find a set of Bible verses that corresponds to your temptation and use them to have a conversation with God about the temptation.

BIBLE STUDY

The Bible is an incredible, life-giving resource. According to the following verses, what does the Bible do for us?

1. Psalm 119:11

2. Psalm 119:24

3. Psalm 119:25

4. Psalm 119:38

5. Psalm 119:45

6. Psalm 119:104

7. Psalm 119:105

8. 2 Timothy 3:16-17

9. Think about the day ahead of you. When will you be most tempted to break your boundaries? Why will you be tempted to break them at that time?

10. Write out a Scripture prayer below with that temptation in mind. You can find Bible verses to pray through by looking at that particular temptation in *I Deserve a Donut* or in one of the lessons in this study that discusses your temptation.

ASSIGNMENT

What is the biggest trial you're going through right now? What emotion are you experiencing? Turn to that section of *I Deserve a Donut* and use the Bible verses to have a conversation with God about your trial.

Day 26

That Looks Tasty

*I*N *I DESERVE a Donut*, I suggested focusing on the taste of food by rating each bite on a scale of 1 to 10. I asked my husband to give this a try one day on the way home from the Dairy Queen just to see what he would say.

My husband is an all-or-nothing kind of guy, so I was fully expecting him to say his whole blizzard was a ten. I was wrong. About halfway through the blizzard, he said, "I'm already at a three. Next time, I'll get a mini." And he did.

Now granted, he's not a compulsive eater. It's easy for him to say no to food. Not so easy for us! Once we get started, it can be difficult to stop.

So what do you do when you're surrounded by good food day in and day out? First, try to focus on the taste of food. And, at least with unhealthy foods, try to stop eating when the taste deteriorates. But what if you do that and you still can't eat your favorite foods with control?

If you find yourself breaking your boundaries again and again with your favorite foods, you may want to consider either limiting them or getting rid of them altogether until you've gotten a little more truth into your system.

I explained how I did this with sweets in *Freedom from Emotional Eating*. First, I gave up all sweets for a month or two. Then I allowed only fruit-based sweets (mainly because I didn't pig-out on them as I did with other sweets). Finally, I allowed all sweets—but only on holidays and social occasions.

It took a couple of years before I could eat sweets on a regular basis without being controlled by them. I knew I was over my addiction the day I threw some cookies in the garbage because they'd been in the freezer too long.

Don't worry if you think you should give up a favorite food but don't have the willpower to do it. That's to be expected. After all, if you were good at following boundaries, you wouldn't be doing this Bible study in the first place!

The question you want to ask yourself is this: Will I have a better chance of following my boundaries if I get rid of my problem foods altogether or if I just try to limit them? Set whatever boundaries you think will be the easiest to follow. Then renew your mind every time you break them.

Just to give you a little hope for the future, I can now have sweets in my house—even on the kitchen counter—and walk by them without batting an eye (well maybe just a little twitch of the eyebrow). You'll be at that point too someday if you continue to renew your mind.

When it comes to our favorite foods, overeating isn't the only thing we need to be careful of. We also need to be careful on a spiritual level. We'll look at that in today's Bible study.

BIBLE STUDY

1. According to the following Bible verses, what do you have to be careful of when you really love something (like food)?

   a. Jeremiah 2:11-13

   b. Isaiah 44:14-17

   c. 1 Corinthians 6:12

2. How do you think you'd know if you loved something too much?

3. What foods do you most often break your boundaries with?

4. Do you think you love those foods too much? Why or why not?

5. Can you think of anything you could do to make it easier to follow your boundaries with those foods?

ASSIGNMENT

1. Rate every bite that goes in your mouth today. Make a note of when the taste deteriorates to an 8.

2. Try to focus on thoroughly enjoying each and every bite.

3. Try to hold your favorite foods with open hands, willing to give them up if necessary.

Day 27

It's My Party and I'll Eat If I Want To

ON'T YOU HATE it when everyone around you is on their fourth piece of pizza and you're sitting there with a salad on your plate? Somehow, it seems unfair. If *they* get four pieces of pizza, we should get four pieces. So we sit there feeling deprived until we can't stand it any longer. Then we eat.

In the back of our minds, a tiny little lie is fueling our actions: *Life should be fair.* And it's not fair if everyone else gets to eat and we don't.

This sounds like the truth. After all, weren't most of us raised by parents who did everything they could to make sure all of us kids were treated equally? And don't we live in a country that tells us every day, in one way or another, that life should be fair?

When we're bombarded with the fairness message everywhere we go, it's hard not to buy into it. In the early years of raising kids and being a homeschool mom, I bought into it hook, line, and sinker. I was constantly writing these three little words in my truth journal: *It's not fair.*

I had no end to the reasons as to why my life wasn't fair. But no matter what the reason, God always gave me the same truth: If He were to line up all the people in the world based on who had the fairest life, *I would be near the top.*

THE FAIRNESS LINE

Think of it. People who are starving in third world countries are on that line. Women who are watching their kids die of AIDS because their husbands were unfaithful are on that line. Kids who have been sold into the sex slave trade are on that line.

And I think it's unfair because someone else gets to have a treat and I don't? The truth never ceases to convict me and bring me to my knees in repentance.

We believe lies like "Life should be fair" because the culture spoon-feeds us those lies from birth. When I write the lies in my journal, I believe them—until I take the time to look at them.

Today I want to encourage you to keep persevering with the renewing of your mind. We're never happy when we're believing the lies of the world. And we'll never break free from our compulsive habits if we don't break free from the lies that fuel those habits.

The truth will set us free but only if we pursue it. Let's do a little pursuing right now.

BIBLE STUDY

1. Have you ever said, "This isn't fair"? When do you usually say it?

2. Is your life really unfair when you think of everything going on all over the world? Why or why not?

3. How does believing the lie that life should be fair and/or that your life is unfair affect the following?

   a. Your emotions

   b. Your weight

   c. Your work

   d. Your relationship with others

   e. Your relationship with God

4. Did Jesus live a fair life? Explain. (Philippians 2:5-11)

5. Does the Bible ever say we should expect to live fair lives? If not, what does it say? (1 John 3:16)

6. The thing I find over and over again in the Bible is that when I do what it asks me to do, with my heart as well as my behavior, I'm always happier—even when it tells me to do hard things. Read Philippians 4:4-12 and list everything we're asked to do in those verses.

7. If you were to list one theme for that passage, what would it be?

8. Do you feel like you're following the theme of that passage when it comes to food and your weight? Why or why not?

9. Spend some time thanking God for your current life, including your current boundaries and weight.

ASSIGNMENT

If you have a social occasion today that involves food (even if it's just a family dinner or snack), pray through the following Bible verses before the occasion so you can focus on the people and not the food: 1 Corinthians 13:4-8, Philippians 2:4, and/or 1 John 3:16. These can also be found in the "Insecurity: Social Situations" section of *I Deserve a Donut.*

Day 28

Worshipping Skinny

WHEN I WAS a child, I loved reading comic books. One of the ads in the comic books showed a scrawny teenage boy running from a bully who had just kicked sand in his face at the beach. The boy signed up for a Charles Atlas weight-lifting program, and three months later he was at the same beach, looking buff and getting revenge on the big bad bully.

I used to love that ad because it was such a success story. I liked seeing that poor little guy get all big and buff. I still love a success story. But now that I'm grown up, I can't help but see the spiritual side of a story like that. From a spiritual perspective, the story's not so great.

Here's why: It leaves God out of the picture.

The boy was desperate. But rather than going to God for help with his problems, he went to the body-building program. The minute he got buff, life was great. The comic books never told us if he was still insecure on the inside.

I hate to say it, but we do the same thing that comic boy did. Instead of going to God to see ourselves through His eyes, we do everything we can to look good in the culture's eyes. This usually manifests itself in one of three ways: 1) we become obsessed with diets, 2) we become obsessed with exercise, or 3) we become obsessed with looking good.

This actually *keeps* us from losing weight. Why? Because

obsession leads to condemnation. We're never skinny enough. We never exercise enough. We never look good enough.

When we do something "bad"—such as majorly breaking our boundaries—we beat ourselves up. Because now *for sure* we'll never be skinny. And since we'll never be skinny, we might as well eat.

If we hold skinny with open hands—willing to never lose weight, content with our body as is—we'll miss out on that whole beating-ourselves-up session. We won't eat in despair because we won't be despairing.

Instead, we'll go calmly to God, renew our minds, and get back on track without a major blowout. Giving up the idol of skinny is essential for both our physical well-being and our spiritual well-being.

BIBLE STUDY

1. We can tell what's important to us by looking at where we spend our free time. List the number of minutes you spend each day on the following activities.

   a. Exercise

   b. Diet (looking for the perfect diet, counting calories, obsessing over what you eat, etc.)

   c. Looks (hair, makeup, shopping, trying on different outfits to see which one looks best, etc.)

   d. Going to God for help with your problems and just to be with Him in prayer and in His Word

2. How would your life change if you were to spend as much time with God as you spend on exercising, dieting, and looking good?

3. According to the following Bible verses, what is the danger of becoming obsessed with things other than God?

   a. 1 Kings 11:1-4

   b. Ecclesiastes 5:10

   c. Mark 10:17-27

   d. 1 Corinthians 6:12

4. Do you think you're making skinny more important than God wants you to make it? Why or why not?

5. Can you think of any lessons God might want to teach you *before* you lose weight?

6. How do you think God wants you to approach weight loss?

ASSIGNMENT

If you struggle with making weight and appearance more important than God wants you to make it, do the greed/lust questions and Bible verses from *I Deserve a Donut* with your goal of losing weight in mind.

Day 29

When You're Not Losing Weight

PICTURE THIS. IT'S Saturday morning, and you've followed your boundaries perfectly all week. Not one little bite off the plan. Nada. You can't wait to step on that old scale. You strip down to your underwear, hold onto the bathroom counter, and gingerly slide onto the scale, careful not to add any extra weight by stepping down too hard.

Then you look at the number on the scale and ...*what???* You can't believe your eyes. Not only did you not lose weight—you *gained* a pound. *Seriously?* Maybe it was a fluke—a scale malfunction. You try again. No fluke. You gained a pound.

So here's my question: What do you do next? Do you say, "Oh well, I'll just keep following my boundaries and hope for a better weigh-in next week"? Or do you say, "I'll *never* lose this weight. Maybe I'm not even *capable* of losing this weight. I might as well GIVE UP!"—and then head to the kitchen for a humungous breakfast?

Here's the funny thing. We eat to escape the trials of regular life. But we also eat to escape the trials of not losing weight. Not exactly efficient, but it's what we do. If we want to lose weight and keep it off, we'll need to learn to go to God for help with our problems, whether they're life-related or food-related.

The truth is, God uses trials to help us grow—even the trial of weight loss. So if we give up and eat, we'll miss out on what He wants to teach us. If you're getting discouraged, please don't give up. Trials aren't fun while you're going through them, but *afterwards* they reap the peaceful fruit of righteousness (Hebrews 12:11). One day you'll be free from the control of food. That will be a peaceful way of life.

If you have a bad weigh-in, renew your mind right away so you aren't tempted to eat in response to the trial. Let's try that right now with today's Bible study. Use the study to work through some aspect of the trial of weight loss, such as not being able to eat what you want, not looking the way you want to look, not being able to stick to your boundaries, not losing weight as quickly as you'd like, or even just continuing to renew your mind day after day.

BIBLE STUDY

Note: This is the same Bible study you did on Day 21. The wonderful thing about the Bible is that it applies to all of life so we can go to it over and over again for different problems.

1. Why do you think this whole weight loss battle is so difficult?

2. What's the hardest part for you?

3. Read Hebrews 12:1-13. Record everything it says about how God wants you to handle this trial and what He's hoping you'll get out of it. Try to make it personal. For example, in verse 1, I might say, "He wants me to lay aside my desire to eat what I want when I want and submit to boundaries even though there are homemade apple caramel muffins with frosting on them in the house *at this very moment.*"

4. How are you currently responding to your weight loss trial?

5. What will happen if you keep doing what you've been doing with this trial?

6. What do you need to change to handle your trial the way God wants you to handle it?

7. What do you think God wants to teach you through this trial? Be specific.

8. When you think of all God could do in your life through this trial, can you see why the whole weight loss battle could be a good thing in your life?

9. What will you need to do if you want to accomplish God's goals for your trial? (Romans 12:1-2; 2 Corinthians 10:3-5)

10. Is there anything you need to change to lose weight and keep it off, either on a practical level or a renewing-of-the-mind level?

ASSIGNMENT

Grab a cozy blanket, curl up in your favorite chair, and spend five minutes praying through the insecurity Bible verses in *I Deserve a Donut* or in the blog post on my blog called "Insecurity Bible verses." As you pray, picture God doing the things He says He'll do in those verses. (Note: This is a repeat of the assignment on Day 12 of this Bible study, but it's so helpful, I'm asking you to do it again!)

Day 30

It's a Journey

I THINK IT WAS the eight cartons of ice cream at my parents' house that started me down the rocky road of emotional eating again. I was doing great until the last day of the visit, and then I let my guard down.

I had no excuse. No, I take that back—I had lots of excuses: *It's a shame to waste this incredible gourmet ice cream...after all, I'm on vacation...I deserve a little splurge on my last day.* I wouldn't necessarily call three bowls of ice cream a little splurge.

Then there was the trip home: *I need to keep up my energy for driving. I'll start being good when I get home.* But I wasn't good. Why? Because the next week was Fair Week. The week our whole town goes to the county fair and indulges in Fair Food: elephant ears, huckleberry milkshakes, chocolate covered bananas, deep-fried Twinkies.

I was bad, bad, bad.

But here's the good news. I only gained a pound or two. Why? Because God was speaking the truth about food to me, even while my mind was speaking lies. I ate more than I should have, but not as much as I would have eaten a couple of years ago. I ate what I felt like eating, but I didn't *feel* like eating as much as I would have a couple of years ago.

Don't get me wrong. I recognize that I was in dangerous territory. Breaking the boundaries consistently is risky. I need them for my own protection. But the victory was that God had changed me so much by that trip I took years ago, that even though the fence was down, I didn't really want to escape.

You'll be at that point too some day if you keep renewing your mind. I know it's hard. I know there are times when you feel like you'll *never ever* change. I felt the same way when I was going through this. You should see how many truth journal entries I have at my house regarding food.

It's been eleven years now since I've broken free from the control of food. I still have troubles with the boundaries at times, but they're minor. Ironically, the time I most feel like breaking them is when I'm writing about weight loss. Instead of being diligent about keeping my boundaries, I think, *I'll just write this Bible study, and when I'm finished, I'll go through it and start being good.*

I never go too far off the path, though, because I've reached the point where I enjoy life *with* boundaries better than life without. And I am a fun-loving, hate-to-be-tied-to-a-schedule person. Maybe you've come to that point, too, but for most people, it takes a lot longer than thirty days.

I encourage you to hang in there. Keep renewing your mind. Do this study over again if it helps. God will help you break free from food's control in your life—but it takes time. While you wait, enjoy your fellowship with Him. We'll end our time together with a look at the journey of weight loss.

BIBLE STUDY

Sometimes when I'm trying to add a new habit to my life or break an old habit, I get so discouraged that I forget to be thankful. Instead of focusing on what God has already done, I focus on how far I still have to go, or on how inept I am in general. I would be far more content if I lived my life in terms of Philippians 4:4-13.

1. Read Philippians 4:4-13 with your weight loss journey in mind. If you lived your life in terms of these verses, how

would you approach weight loss (and life)? List as many things from these verses as you can.

Isn't it interesting how the Bible can completely change your mindset? After writing the last question, I answered it for myself with my writing struggles in mind. God used the Scriptures to completely change my attitude.

Instead of focusing on my writing woes, I focused on all the blessings God has given me, including His great love and kindness. There are so many blessings to be found when we go looking for them. We just need to take the time to look.

Praying with thanksgiving helps us focus on God's goodness rather than life's badness. Paul tells us how to do it in Philippians 4:6: Ask God for help, then start thanking Him. This is different than those prayers where we spend all of our time asking and none of our time thanking.

Thankfulness helps us break out of our self-absorbed rut and look at life from God's perspective. Because of that, it's a great way to renew our minds. Let's give it a try with weight loss.

2. First, ask God for what you want (to lose weight). Then start thanking Him for everything you can think of to thank Him for. Thank Him for what He's done, for what He's going to do, and for all that He is: loving, kind, powerful, compassionate, full of truth, full of mercy and grace, majestic, creative, holy—the list could go on and on. If you run out of

things to thank Him for, look at Appendix D for ideas. Go ahead and write your prayer in the space below.

3. Why do you think praying with thanksgiving is so powerful?

As you continue to work on breaking free from the control of food, try to be thankful. Especially on those days when everything seems to be going wrong and you feel like you'll never ever break free from the control of food.

You *will* break free. Believe that! God is powerful, and He will transform you. It just takes a heavy dose of truth and time. My prayer is that you will continue to renew your mind as you go to Him for help with food and life. I'm excited to see what He will do!

ASSIGNMENT

1. Make a plan: What will you do after you finish this Bible study to continue working on breaking free from the control of food and drawing closer to God?

2. Continue trying to see yourself as God sees you. And always remember: You don't have to be skinny to be beautiful. *You are already beautiful!!!*

Boundaries

ECAUSE THIS BOOK is focused more on *how* to follow your boundaries rather than on the boundaries themselves, I haven't included much information on the different types of boundaries available. You'll be able to find that information in books written by people who advocate for their particular set of boundaries (low-carb, intuitive eating, calorie plans, etc.).

You may decide to use one set of boundaries to lose weight and another set to maintain it, or you may want to use the same boundaries for both losing and maintaining. Here are three of the most common types of lifelong boundaries that people tell me they use:

HUNGER/SATISFACTION OR INTUITIVE EATING

With these boundaries, you limit how often you eat by hunger—in other words, eat only when you're hungry and stop when you're satisfied.

The advantage of this plan is that you can eat whenever you're hungry, and it's a natural way to control your weight.

The disadvantage is that you may not be hungry when you want to be hungry (like when all your friends are going out for ice cream or when your family is sitting down to dinner).

If you choose this option, you'll have to learn how to plan your meals and snacks so that you're hungry when you want to be.

MEALS AND SNACKS

Another way to limit eating is to have a set number of meals and snacks each day. This is what I do. My boundaries are three meals a day and a snack only if I'm really hungry or it's a social occasion.

The advantage of this is that it fits easily into life. You can eat with your family and also have a snack available for those unexpected eating occasions.

The disadvantage is that it's not a guarantee of weight loss and maintenance. You could gain weight on three meals and a snack if your meals and snacks are too big.

If you choose this option, you'll need to have a general idea of how much you can eat and still maintain your weight. If you're hungry for every meal and snack, you're probably eating the right amount.

You'll also need to plan what you're going to eat *before* you sit down. If you eat something you didn't plan on eating (a second helping, for example), consider that a breaking of the boundaries and renew your mind.

POINTS OR CALORIES

Another way to limit eating is to count Weight Watchers points or calories. The advantage of this system is that you know exactly what you're eating.

The disadvantage is that you have to go to all the work of counting the points and calories, and if you're a perfectionist, you could become obsessed with points and calories. If this is your tendency, think about choosing one of the other options.

HOW TO CHOOSE BOUNDARIES

If you're having a hard time deciding which boundaries to choose, ask yourself this question: *What can I live with for the rest of my life?* Your boundaries should be loose enough that you can live with them on a permanent basis but strict enough that you won't be able to eat just for fun or emotional reasons.

Think about your lifestyle, eating preferences, and health concerns when setting up your boundaries, and be sure to talk to your doctor first if you have medical issues.

If you're a perfectionist, you might be thinking, *I need to find the perfect set of boundaries if I want this to work!* This isn't true because we're transformed by the renewing of the mind, not by finding the perfect boundaries. Just choose a set of boundaries and give it a try. You can always try different boundaries later if you think that would be more helpful. If you'd like more information on the different types of boundaries available, check out the weight loss section at your local library.

Boundaries Questions

If you're having a hard time making a decision about which boundaries to use, try these questions to explore the decision. Just keep in mind that you can always change your boundaries later if you decide another set will work better.

1. Why are you having a hard time making this decision?

2. Do you have enough information to make a good decision? If not, what information do you need to gather?

3. Is it possible to choose a perfect set of boundaries that will be easy to follow in every situation? Why or why not?

4. What do you think will happen if you don't choose any boundaries?

5. What are your options for boundaries?

6. Which set of boundaries would fit into your lifestyle the best, if any? Explain.

7. Would one set of boundaries be easier to follow than another? If so, which one?

8. What boundaries would you be willing to live with for the rest of your life, if any?

9. Do you think God would prefer one choice over another? If so, why?

10. Are you choosing this set of boundaries because it's expected of you, or do you actually think this is a good set of boundaries for you?

11. Is this one of those situations where you can't really know what's best?

12. What's the worst thing that can happen if you make what appears to be the wrong decision?

13. Can you change your boundaries later if you decide another set would work better?

14. What will have to accept to make this decision and not keep second-guessing yourself?

15. What can you thank God for in this situation? (Note: Once you make your decision, focus on being thankful for the good things about the option you chose.)

Appendix C

Renewing of the Mind Questions

Note: These questions are meant to help you develop a renewing-the-mind habit. If you already have an established habit and just don't feel like renewing your mind one day, ask yourself, "What emotion am I experiencing?" and then renew your mind with that set of questions and verses.

INDULGENCE
I don't feel like renewing my mind.

1. Why don't you feel like renewing your mind?

2. Why do you want to establish a renewing-the-mind habit? Be specific.

3. Is it easy to develop habits? Why or why not?

4. How often will you renew your mind if you only do it when you feel like doing it?

5. What sacrifices will you have to make to renew your mind today?

6. If you want to develop a renewing-the-mind habit, will you eventually have to make the sacrifice to work on it?

7. If so, what would be the advantage of getting started right now?

8. What will your life look like a few months down the road if you persevere daily with this habit?

9. What can you thank God for in this situation?

LACK OF IMPORTANCE
It's not a big deal if I don't do this today.

1. Why don't you feel like renewing your mind?

2. Why do you want to develop a renewing-the-mind habit? Be specific.

3. Why do you feel like it's not important to work on it today?

4. Do you think God wants you to meet with Him today? Why or why not?

5. Do you think Satan wants you to meet with God today? Why or why not?

6. What will your life look like a few months down the road if you persevere daily with this habit?

7. What can you thank God for in this situation?

PROCRASTINATION
I'll do it later.

1. Why don't you feel like renewing your mind?

2. Why do you want to develop a renewing-the-mind habit?

3. Why do you want to put it off until later?

4. In the past, have you been good at renewing your mind later? If not, what usually happens?

5. Is this one of those things where the longer you put it off, the more you'll dread it?

6. What are you dreading most about it?

7. Can you break the process down into smaller, less intimidating steps?

8. What is one thing you could do right now that you wouldn't dread?

9. Why don't you try doing that and see if it helps to jumpstart you? If it doesn't, try praying through a couple of the renewing of the mind Bible verses. If you're still having problems, try some of the other sets of renewing-the-mind questions.

REWARD

I don't want to make the effort if I can't guarantee success.

1. Why don't you feel like renewing your mind?

2. Why do you want to develop a renewing-the-mind habit?

3. Do you think God wants you to develop this habit? Why or why not?

4. If so, what would His reasons be?

5. Are His reasons different than your reasons? If so, how are they different?

6. Can you guarantee that God will give you what you want (weight loss, freedom from your negative emotions, etc.) if you make the sacrifice to renew your mind?

7. Would His fellowship during the process be a reward even if you don't get what you want?

8. Is there anything you need to trust Him with?

9. Is there anything you need to accept?

10. What can you thank God for in this situation?

LACK OF TIME
I'm too busy.

1. Why do you feel like you can't renew your mind today?

2. How much time would it take to do it?

3. Which of the following is true:

    a. You really don't have time to renew your mind.

    b. You could make the time, but you'd rather not.

    c. You're an all-or-nothing person, and if you can't do it the way you want to do it, you'd rather not do it at all.

    d. You dread the thought of renewing your mind, and time is a good excuse.

4. If you're really busy today, could you still squeeze out five minutes to renew your mind?

5. What would be the value of spending five minutes on it?

6. If you don't follow through on your commitment today, will it be harder to do tomorrow? Why or why not?

7. Is there anything you could do today to help make it easier to renew your mind tomorrow? If so, what could you do?

8. If this is an ongoing problem, would it be possible to make some time to renew your mind by cutting down on some of your other activities?

9. If so, what could you cut out of your schedule to allow time to renew your mind?

LACK OF TIME (HARD-CORE VERSION)
I don't have time to meet with God.

1. In the past 48 hours, how much time have you spent in the following activities? Be specific.

   a. Facebook

   b. YouTube

   c. Television

   d. Texting

   e. Computer games

   f. Hobbies

   g. Recreational activities

   h. Hanging out with friends

   i. Exercise

   j. Reading

   k. Wandering around your house or apartment

   l. Work that isn't required to support yourself and/or your family

2. Would it be possible to make some time to renew your mind by cutting down on some of your other activities?

3. If so, what could you cut out of your schedule to allow time to renew your mind?

4. Is there any reason you couldn't start renewing your mind right now?

5. If not, why don't you go ahead and get started?

BIBLE VERSES

Isaiah 62:4a, 5b It will no longer be said to you, "Forsaken," Nor to your land will it any longer be said, "Desolate"; But you will be called, "My delight is in her," And your land, "Married"; for the Lord delights in you, and as the bridegroom rejoices over the bride, so your God will rejoice over you.

Jeremiah 29:13 You will seek Me and find Me when you search for Me with all your heart.

Jeremiah 31:3-4 The Lord appeared to him from afar, saying, "I have loved you with an everlasting love; therefore I have drawn you with lovingkindness. Again I will build you and you will be rebuilt, O virgin of Israel! Again you will take up your tambourines, and go forth to the dances of the merrymakers."

John 15:4 Abide in Me, and I in you. As the branch cannot bear fruit of itself unless it abides in the vine, so neither can you unless you abide in Me.

Romans 12:2 And do not be conformed to this world, but be transformed by the renewing of your mind, so that you may prove what the will of God is, that which is good and acceptable and perfect.

Galatians 5:16 But I say, walk by the Spirit, and you will not carry out the desire of the flesh.

Galatians 6:9 Let us not lose heart in doing good, for in due time we will reap if we do not grow weary.

2 Corinthians 10:3-5 For though we walk in the flesh, we do not war according to the flesh, for the weapons of our warfare are not of the flesh, but divinely powerful for the destruction of fortresses. We are destroying speculations and every lofty thing raised up against the knowledge of God, and we are taking every thought captive to the obedience of Christ.

Hebrews 12:11 All discipline for the moment seems not to be joyful, but sorrowful; yet to those who have been trained by it, afterwards it yields the peaceful fruit of righteousness.

Things to Thank God For

1. That we can do all things through Him. Psalm 18:28-29; Philippians 4:13

2. That He will complete the work He began in us. Philippians 1:6

3. That He makes all things work together for good, even failure. Romans 8:28

4. That when God allows bad things to happen, He always has a plan for redemption. Hebrews 12:10-11; James 1:2-4, 12; 1 Peter 5:9-10; Romans 8:28; Jeremiah 29:11-13

5. That our suffering won't last forever. Psalm 30:5; Psalm 71:20; Jeremiah 31:13, 17

6. That God is good even when life isn't. Psalm 27; 63; 34:8; 59:16-17

7. That even suffering can be good. Philippians 3:8-12; 1 Peter 3:13-17; 4:1-2

8. That life is about God, not about creating the perfect life. Philippians 1:21; 3:7-8; 4:11-12; James 1:17

9. That God understands what we're going through and wants to help. Hebrews 4:15-16

10. That God will take care of us. Psalm 73:23-24; Isaiah 41:17-18; Lamentations 3:22-25; Philippians 4:19

11. His power. Psalm 73:26; Isaiah 44:6-8; 1 John 4:4

12. His presence. Psalm 46:1-3, 7; Isaiah 43:2-7; John 14:16-19

13. His Word. Psalm 119

14. His love. Isaiah 62:4-5; Zephaniah 3:17; Romans 8:35, 38-39

15. His peace. Philippians 4:6-7; John 14:27

16. His protection. Psalm 27:1-5; 46:1-2, 7; 61:1-2; 63:7-8; Matthew 11:28

17. His compassion and understanding. Psalm 34:18; Matthew 9:36; Hebrews 2:17-18; 4:15-16

18. All He has done for us in the past. Psalm 77:11-15

19. All He will do for us in the future. John 14:1-3, 18-19; 2 Corinthians 4:17; Philippians 4:6-7

20. That He is enough. Psalm 63:7-8; 73:25; Daniel 3:16-18; 2 Corinthians 4:8-9; 9:8; Philippians 1:21; 3:7-8; 4:11-13; Hebrews 12:28-29

Other Resources by Barb Raveling

Podcasts:

- *Taste for Truth*—a Christian weight-loss podcast
- *Christian Habits Podcast*

Books:

- *Freedom from Emotional Eating*—a weight-loss Bible Study
- *I Deserve a Donut (And Other Lies That Make You Eat)*
- *Renewing of the Mind Project*
- Personal growth Bible study coming January, 2018

Apps:

- *I Deserve a Donut (and Other Lies That Make You Eat)* available for Android and iOS

You can also find information on these resources at Barb's blog at barbraveling.com.

LEADER'S GUIDE

If you'd like to teach *Taste for Truth* to a group, you can download a free leader's guide at barbraveling.com under the Podcasts and Resources tab.

About the Author

BARB HAS BEEN writing and teaching classes on weight loss for the last eleven years. She blogs and podcasts about breaking free from habits and strongholds through the renewing of the mind at barbraveling.com. She and her husband live in Montana and have four adult children. They like to hike, backpack, read, go on walks, and hang out with family and friends in their spare time.

Made in the USA
San Bernardino, CA
12 January 2020

63099491R00095